Eyewitness Accounts of Slavery in the Danish West Indies

also
**Graphic Tales
of Other Slave Happenings
on Ships and Plantations**

Isidor Paiewonsky

*Best wishes
Paiewonsky*

**Fordham University Press
New York
1989**

Dedicated to my wife
Charlotte
with love

I.P.

LC 89-84742
ISBN 0-8232-1259-9 (clothbound)
ISBN 0-8232-1260-2 (paperback)

Manufactured in the United States of America by Aristographics Inc.
Designed by Barry Eisenberg

Foreword

The archives of European countries, Great Britain, France, Holland, Spain and Portugal, are heavy with documents dealing with the participation of these countries in the African slave trade during the 17th, 18th, and 19th centuries.

Many books and histories have been written in various languages with the British outstripping all others in its graphic accounts of the trade.

Outside of the work of the Danish-American historian, Waldemar Westergaard (1917), little was known or written about the Danish participation and it was considerable. Westergaard summed it up this way:

"At first the Danish Company tried to make use of the dregs of the white population of Copenhagen to work on its West India plantations. These Danish immigrants died off like flies. They were unable to withstand conditions in the tropics.

"This lead to the establishment by Denmark of barracks, or barracoons, defended by forts on the west coast of Africa where Negro slaves could be collected for transport to the West Indies."

The purpose of this book is to attempt to reveal the extent of this Danish involvement.

I.P.

Waldemar Westergaard

About forty years ago it was my good fortune to come upon the scholarly work of Waldemar Westergaard, *The Danish West Indies under Company Rule.*

Historically, this is an important work. It was the first history of the Danish West Indies written in English in which the subject matter was taken directly from primary Danish manuscripts.

Waldemar Westergaard was well suited for the job. Born in the United States, the son of a Danish family which immigrated to North Dakota, Waldemar spoke and read Danish fluently.

A history major, Westergaard received his training at the University of California. Going through some intriguing old Danish manuscripts in the Bancroft Collection (University of California), Westergaard was struck by the way historians in general, and Danish historians in particular, had neglected the history of the Danish West Indies.

Westergaard decided to do an in-depth study of Denmark's West Indian experience (1671-1917) as a thesis for his doctorate. Taking a leave of absence from his position as assistant professor of history at Pomona College, California, Westergaard went to Copenhagen and spent a year of intensive research in the Danish State Archives (Rigsarkivet).

While gathering material for his book, Westergaard made a detailed list of the historical material which he handled. He incorporated this list into his book (see bibliography, pages 263-283), twenty pages of solid, invaluable historical sources. Moreover, Westergaard indicated the exact places where such material could be found. For instance:

"The chief repository of first hand material dealing with the

Danish West India and Guinea Company is the Danish State Archives (Rigsarkivet) in Copenhagen. The official records of the Company are piled high on the shelves of the topmost story of the Archives building, where their repose has rarely been disturbed."

As if to make sure that a researcher interested in Denmark's West Indian and African history got maximum coverage, Westergaard directs the researcher to the Peder Mariager manuscript (page 267 of the bibliography):

Peder Mariager : Een saavidt mueligt fuldstoendig Historisk Efterretning extraheret af Det Vestindiske og Guineske Compagnies Archiv, Boger og Protocoller, angaaende bemelte Compagnies Etablissementer udi Vestindien og Guinea, fra begyndelsen....

This Mariager manuscript (222 pages, dated at the Company's office, July 30, 1753), constitutes the official account of the Company's activities from its establishment in 1671 up to within a year or so of its dissolution (mid-18th century):

"Peder Mariager had been employed in the Company's office as a bookkeeper (upwards of 30 years), and was intimately acquainted with its affairs. His manuscript is written with remarkable accuracy...."

Over the years, this writer has made good use of the Westergaard list. With the help of Danish and Norwegian scholars, skilled translators and helpful archivists, a large portion of the material used in the following volume, *Eyewitness Accounts of Slavery in the Danish West Indies*, has been researched, translated and condensed from sources indicated by Westergaard.

I.P.

Slave traders attacking a Negro village (Courtesy Mapes Monde Co. Ltd., Rome)

Frederiksberg was situated 1130 yards east of Cabo Corso. Since it was not possible to build a harbor, the Danes got permission to go into Cabo Corso harbor to load and unload their vessels there. Because of very dangerous anchorage and very heavy seas, they had to stay aboard their ships until the Negroes came to pick them up in their canoes.

The Danes worked closely with the Fetus and other neighboring tribes such as the Akwamu and the Akim.

The Danes paid monthly rent and had to give presents to the tribal leaders. They also paid the Fetus duty on all goods imported from Europe. The Fetu chieftains received the first piece of every kind of goods.

The Danes had their "ups" and "downs" during the latter part of the 17th century and at times, they were mostly "downs." The Dutch harassed them at every turn and finally attacked the Danish fortification at Frederiksberg, plundered it, and burnt it down.

A blacksmith, one Jans Jacob Zur-eich, a native of Zurich, Switzerland, arrived at Frederiksberg in the year 1659. He saw the fighting between the Dutch and the Danes and he was eye-witness to much Dutch brutality. After nine years of service with the Danes and many experiences, he returned to Hamburg and then to Zurich where he published a book: *African-sche Reiszle in die Landshaft Fetu Chreibum*. He described life at Frederiksberg and the living of the natives in great detail.

Another author, Wilhelm Johan Muller, a Hamburg minister, was employed by the Danish Company in 1661 and stayed on the Guinea Coast for eight years. He was the first minister sent out under the Danish flag. His book was published in 1676 under the title: *Die Africansche auf der Guineischen Gold Coast gelegene Laudschaff Fetu*.

After the loss of Frederiksberg, the Danes concentrated their holdings and activities at Christiansborg. They were much weakened by the losses caused by the Dutch as well as by devastating illnesses among the Danish survivors. Christiansborg was built on bought land on a cliff close to the coast with consistently rough seas. It was even more difficult to land by Christiansborg than by Cabo Corso.

It is estimated by Danish historians that their ships carried

Official Seal of the Danish West India and Guinea Company (Courtesy The Danish State Archives, Denmark)

Guinea Coast map, engraved by R.W. Seale 1700 (*Churchill's Collection of Voyages and Travels London*, 1756) Arrows indicate Danish settlements

View of Fort Fredericksberg from the sea, western approach

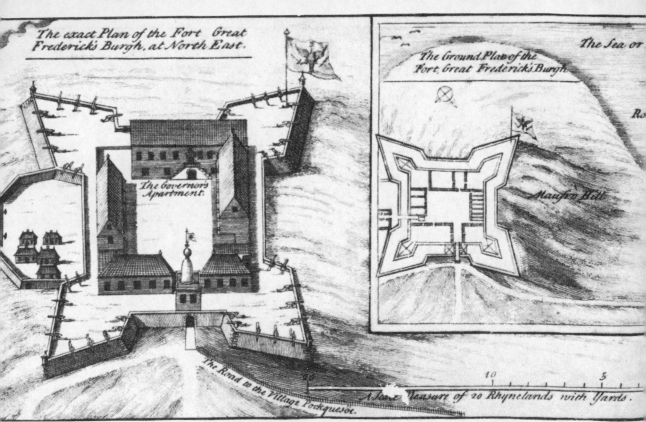

Ground plan of Fort Fredericksberg (Courtesy Danish State Archives, Denmark)

(Top) Fort Christianborg at Accra (*Churchill's Collection of Voyages and Travels*, London, 1756) *Inset* A rendering of the Courtyard, Fort Christianborg by J.V. Svedstrup Kgl. (Royal Library's Collection of Prints, Denmark)

but a fraction of the total number of slaves transported. In retrospect, it was not worth the stigma nor the trouble. It did not produce profits and it cost many Danish lives. As it was, the Danish colonies had been able to buy their slaves cheaper from the Dutch, the British, or the interlopers.

It was not until the latter part of the 17th century that the Danish King and the West India and Guinea Company tried to reactivate the Guinea trade with a positive emphasis on slave trading. To quote directly from archive sources:

"Suddenly it seemed a good idea to send Danish ships with Danish merchandise to Guinea and from there with slaves to the West Indies and from there on home to Denmark with West Indian goods . . .

"The necessity to get black labor for St. Thomas in the West Indies which the Danish West India and Guinea Company had taken over spoke strongly for using the three cornered routes and make the slave trade the main point in the Company's activities.

"There were no moral scruples at this point. Everybody involved wanted to make a profit . . ."

In trying to explain the involvement of the Danish Court and the Danish West India and Guinea Company in the slave trade, Danish historians point to a widely held concept of many monarchs and capitalists of the 17th and early 18th centuries. It was the concept that trading in slaves meant huge profits. It was believed to be the best way to bail out near bankrupt colonial companies that were operating constantly in the red and showing no dividends or returns to stockholders.

According to Westergaard:

"It was during the Governorship of Johan Lorentz (1694-1702) when St. Thomas began to be administered as a normal, well-ordered colony that the Directors were able to carry out a plan for direct participation in the slave trade with ships owned by the Company. It was not until 1733, after the Company had suffered a number of severe losses at sea, and about the time it began negotiations for the purchase of St. Croix from France, that it was ready to let the slave trade fall back into private hands. . . ."

The sea losses, mentioned by Westergaard, are important

because, occurring as they did within a period of four or five years, they almost broke the financial back of the Danish West India and Guinea Company. The records show the losses occurred at a time when the Company was becoming more and more involved in the slave trade. Actually the Company had assigned large, well-equipped ships to the business in the hope of developing substantial profits.

Danish archivists tell us that on April 25, 1699, the *Christianus Quintus* sailed from Christiansborg, West Africa, for St. Thomas with a load of 549 slaves, 295 men, 254 women plus 61 elephant tusks which weighed a total of 2,371 pounds. The ship also carried gold and gold dust at a value of 2,488 rix dollars.

On July 29, 1700, the *Fredericus Quartus* left Christiansborg for St. Thomas with 542 slaves and 7,185 pounds of ivory. After this, there were frequent sailings of these two specially equipped slave ships carrying substantial loads of slaves, ivory, and gold to St. Thomas. Prospects looked good.

Tragedy struck in 1705 and it happened to one of the largest ships of the Danish slave fleet. After considerable delay due to the tribal wars that were raging, *The Cron-Printzen* left Christiansborg for St. Thomas with a load of 820 slaves, 460 men and 360 women, the largest number of slaves ever to leave on one Danish ship from Guinea for St. Thomas. Before the departure, smallpox broke out. Many died on board.

From Christiansborg, *The Cron-Printzen* went to Principe, an island in the Gulf of Guinea, to get provisions, but here a fire started in the ship's gunpowder room and the ship exploded. Only five men were saved.

The other ship tragedies occurred in 1709-1710. To quote from the archivists:

"From November 28, 1708 to April 1, 1709, the violent and blood thirsty chief of the Akwamu tribe, Aquando, had laid seige to the provincial capital at Accra. During this period, he ruined four Negro towns: Orsu, near Christiansborg, and Labadi, Tossing and Ningo, further towards the east, destroying inhabitants of Accra by the thousands and taking many prisoners. The Accras fled to Christiansborg and asked for protection but the factor there stayed neutral and watched the

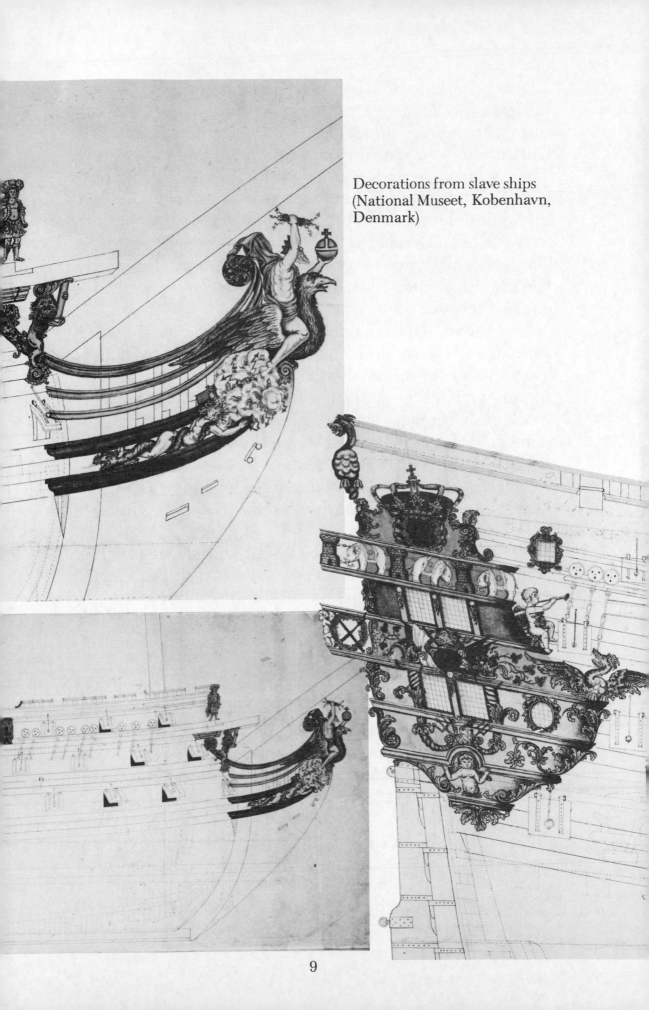

Decorations from slave ships
(National Museet, Kobenhavn,
Denmark)

Accras being killed and captured in large numbers.

"It was under these conditions that the two big Company ships *Christianus Quintus* and *Fredericus Quartus* arrived in Christiansborg on April 16 and April 25, 1709, respectively. There was a large amount of gold at the fort and 8000 pounds of ivory but because of the closeness of the tribal war, a considerable delay occurred in the loading of the ships.

"Finally on October 2, 1709, both ships departed for St. Thomas. The *Fredericus Quartus* had 435 slaves aboard, the *Christianus Quintus*, 334. The large load of gold was divided equally between the 2 ships.

"But the voyage was haunted with bad luck. First the winds were against the ships. They got lost and bypassed St. Thomas. They got into the western part of the Caribbean sea where the stream forced them south. The slaves were put ashore on the coast of Nicaragua and after mutiny aboard, the crew plundered the gold boxes. On March 7, 1710, they left the ships in life boats.

"The *Fredericus Quartus* burned the following night. The *Christianus Quintus* went ashore where the waves splintered her...."

Two very revealing narratives dealing with slave conditions at the Guinea "factories" and aboard the slave ships appeared in the year 1788. Both books were written by ship doctors, one Danish, the other British. Both men wrote from a wealth of first-hand experience and what they had to say had a profound effect on the public at the time.

The Danish work, *Reise nach Guinea und den Carabaischen Inseln. Von Guinea nach Westindien. Zusland eines sklavenschiffes*, was authored by P. E. Isert who had been chief physician in the Danish "factory" in Guinea and who had served for several years as surgeon aboard the slave ships on the Atlantic crossing.

Isert presented a vivid and detailed description of the handling of slaves from the time they were received and "processed" at Christiansborg, West Africa, until they reached their destination, St. Thomas, West Indies.

"As the slaves were brought in by the tribal captors," noted Isert, "they were sold on a barter basis to the factors of the forts

Bay of Principe where the *Cron-Printzen* blew up. From John Barbot's description of the coasts of Guinea (*Churchill's Voyages and Travels*, London, 1756)

and then housed and guarded by their new owners in sheds or warehouses, known as barracoons, until the arrival of the slave ships."

In the Dutch and British barracoons, those purchased, "were set aside for branding with a hot iron on the breast or the shoulder with the identifying mark of the company or the individual purchaser."

Whenever possible, the Danes tried to avoid or dispense with this "branding process." In most cases the entire cargo was consigned to one proprietor only, the Danish West India and Guinea Company in St. Thomas, so there was little need to separate or differentiate the cargo. In the event that the Danes had to "brand," the operation was performed carefully with pieces of silver wire, heated just hot enough to blister without burning the skin.

The British work was written by Alexander Falconbridge and was entitled *Account of the Slave Trade on the Coast of Africa.* Because the British traffic in slaves was on a much greater scale than the Danish, the horrors, the brutality, and the sicknesses that occurred under the British flag made the Danish effort seem trivial by comparison.

Falconbridge's book was translated into Danish and received wide circulation in Denmark. In fact, it became a much quoted source for the reform group founded in July 1791 and headed by Count Ernst Schimmelmann, a prominent Danish capitalist of the time. Schimmelmann was director and a heavy investor in a Danish company directly involved in the African slave traffic, but he was morally opposed to it and worked for its abolition.

Regardless of nationalities, there was an overall similarity in the settlements, the manner and techniques of building, of trading and the methods of preparation for the "middle passage," the term applied to the movement of slaves across the Atlantic.

The horrors of the Middle Passage from the Guinea Coast to the West Indies showed no preference. Captives, whether they be persons of authority uprooted from the great tribes of Accra, Dahomey, Ashanti, Loango, El Mina, Calabar, and others; kings, queens, warriors, statesmen, were crammed into

Slaves brought in by their captors (E. Forbes, Dahomey, London, 1851)

Slave auction (P.E. Isert, *Reise nach Guinea*, Kobenhavn, 1788)

Guinea Coast natives preparing ivory for shipment (Frederick V. Atlas Kgl. Biblisteks Kortsamling)

the tightly confining holds of the slave ships together with the many wretched captives already accustomed to servitude and tribal slavery.

Victims, the mighty and the lowly, all were exposed to the humiliation of the "middle passage" and suffered terribly. Ill fed and jammed into space in which it was impossible to sit or stand, no light, air, sanitation, wracked by frightful diseases, it was little wonder that many died in transit.

In his narrative, *Reise nach Guinea und den Carabaischen Inseln*, P. E. Isert, the Danish physician, tells of the indignities to which Negro women slaves were subject at the hands of the ship's officers and crewmen during the crossing from Africa to St. Thomas.

Many of these officers and crewmen were outcasts at home, convicts released from the Copenhagen jails, bankrupts, or plain rejects from a Danish society eager to get rid of them. With most opportunities closed to them at home, it was little wonder that they were willing to go to the coast of Africa where they, and other European outcasts like them, as one historian put it:

"... could lead a life of indolence, with little or no restraint.

Slaves being brought in by their captors (Courtesy The Granger Collection New York)

There they might indulge nearly every human passion with utter freedom, whether it be confirmed drunkenness or unrestrained intercourse with Negro girls. They knew that the deadly climate was likely to claim them, so it was a 'short life and a merry one' for many of these outcasts. . . ."

It was little wonder that the degree of bestiality and debauchery aboard the slavers on their way to St. Thomas reached the height described by Isert. The monotony of a long voyage, bad food, access to the rum casks, captive women, naked and permissive, all were factors that led to uncontrolled orgies.

Nor was this bestiality and debauchery limited to the Danish slavers. Slave history is full of similar orgies on the ocean crossings and no nation was exempted.

Orgies and debauchery aboard the slave ships continued right down to the 19th century. In fact, the bestiality seemed to increase after slavery had been declared illegal by most of the European nations and the traffic had been taken over by a group of desperate and brutal men who ran the blockade. Captain Richard Drake, notorious slave smuggler, gives the following account of a voyage on the illegal Brazilian slaver, *Gloria*:

"Once off the coast, the ship became half-bedlam and half-brothel. Our Captain and his two mates set an example of reckless wickedness. They stripped themselves and danced with the slave wenches while our crazy cook played the fiddle. There was little attempt at discipline and rum and lewdness reigned supreme. . . ."

****

As a result of all this ghastly business that occurred on the slave ships, particularly during the 18th century, the graveyards of St. Thomas hold many a forgotten sailor and ship's officer, debilitated by scurvy and debauchery on the "middle passage" and finished off by excesses in the grog shops that abounded in Charlotte Amalia at that time.

Sources

1. Waldemar Westergaard, *The Danish West Indies Under Company Rule, 1671-1754* (New York: 1917).

2. Records of the Danish West Indies and Guinea Company, Danish State Archives (Copenhagen, Denmark).

3. Peter Mariager Manuscript, 1753, Danish State Archives (Copenhagen, Denmark).

4. Governor Johan Lorentz Journals and Letters to Directors, Danish West Indies and Guinea Company, 1694-1702. Danish State Archives (Copenhagen, Denmark).

5. Jans Jacob Zureich, *Africansche Reiszle in die Landshaft Fetu Chreibum* (Zurich: 1674).

6. Wilhelm Johan Muller, *De Africansche auf der Guineischen Gold Coast Fetu* (Hamburg: 1676).

7. Paul Erdmann Isert, *Reise nach Guinea und den Carabaischen Inseln* (Copenhagen: 1788).

8. Voregamle Tropekolonier. *De Danske Etablissementer paa Guinea Kysten 1671-1754*, Westermann's Forlag (Copenhagen: 1952).

Frontispiece of P.E. Isert's *Reise nach Guinea . . .* (Kobenhavn, Denmark, 1788)

II

Dr. Paul Erdmann Isert
His Background and Letters

According to Westergaard, Paul Erdmann Isert had been chief physician in the Danish settlement in Guinea (Christiansborg), and had served for a time on slave ships plying between Africa and the Danish West Indies, St. Thomas, and St. Croix.

Isert wrote a series of letters from the African Guinea Coast and the West Indies to family and friends in Denmark telling of his experiences. Letter 12 is headed: *Reise von Guinea nach Westindien. Zustand eines Sklavenschiffes. Rebellion der Sklaven. Beschreibung von St. Croix.*

Collected and published in Copenhagen in the year 1788, and gathering dust on the Archive shelves for almost two centuries, Paul Erdmann Isert's letters were translated into English by a Norwegian scholar and friend, Ulf Renberg, feature writer for the Scandinavian newspaper, *Arbeiderbladet*, Oslo, Norway.

I.P.

In the year 1756, a child, Paul Erdmann Isert, was born into a prominent mercantile family in Brandenburg, Germany. Thirty years later, this young man was offering ideas to important people in Europe that, if followed, might have changed the course of West Indian history.

The exact date when the Isert family emigrated from Germany to Denmark is not known. What is known is that Paul Erdmann Isert was given an excellent education in the Danish academies, and that in the year 1783, at the age of 27, he left Denmark for the royal possession in Guinea (Africa), with a title as royal medical officer.

Shortly after his arrival in Africa, and because of shortages of medical staff resulting from epidemics and deaths, Isert assumed the position as chief physician in the Danish Hospital in Guinea. Later, he served as medical officer on slave ships carrying human cargoes from the African coast to the Danish West Indies.

Between 1783 and 1787, Isert wrote a series of remarkable letters to family and important friends in Europe. He described the flora and fauna of the Guinea coast in detail, and the problems and human patterns of European and native behavior in the little known Danish settlement there. But above all, he presented a graphic and valuable eyewitness account of the dark and inhuman side of the slave trade, the agonies and horrors of the Middle Passage, and his ideas for drastic reform.

Isert's letters created considerable interest in Denmark. They were collected and published in Copenhagen in 1788 under the title *Reise nach Guinea und den Carabaischen Inseln*.

In one of his letters from Christiansted, St. Croix, to his father in Denmark, dated March 12, 1787, Isert described an uprising on a slave ship in which he was almost killed:

"I am still alive, dear Father, after another long sea voyage, but I have been very close to death. We left the coast of Africa, October 7, 1786, aboard the ship, *Christiansborg* with the West Indies as our destination.

"Try to imagine the commotion aboard a slave ship, built originally to carry 200 people and now crammed with 452 slaves, kept in line by 36 Europeans. Imagine the sight of these unhappy people, prisoners of war, or for some other reason, who have been sold to Europeans and are now being taken in chains from their native lands and homes to a country they do not even know. Impossible that they can expect something good from the future, since the Europeans are using such violent means in dealing with them.

"In their homelands, the most terrible rumors circulated about the use of slaves in the West Indies; to such an extent that these captive people are terrified.

"A slave once asked me if the shoes I was wearing had been made from Negro-skin. He could see, he said, that they had the same color. Others believe that we eat Negroes and make powder from their bones. They cannot believe that they are only to be used for field labour, since from their experiences, field labour takes such little time and occupy so few hands.

"Therefore, they do not believe what the Europeans say, that they are going to a wonderful country. They use any and every opportunity to run away or to kill themselves. They fear death less than slavery in the West Indies. . . .

"One has to use the greatest forethought to prevent them from ending their days. Captains on French ships do not allow them to carry a ribbon of linen, fearing that they will hang themselves with it, which several have done.

"The terrible treatment these unhappy people suffer under barbaric skippers and crews, often cause them to conspire against the powers that be. Usually these conspiracies take place in the harbour before departure, or during the first days while the ship is still close to the African coast.

"During my stay in Guinea, I have seen several such sad examples. In 1785, the slaves aboard a Dutch ship rebelled the day they were to leave for the West Indies. They overpowered and killed the Europeans, except for a young ship's boy who had saved himself by climbing up the main-mast.

"Before the whites succumbed completely, they had succeeded in firing several distress guns, heard on shore. Canoes with soldiers and armed free-Negroes were sent to help them.

"As soon as the rebelling slaves saw them coming and knew that they would be overcome, they decided to kill themselves. One of them ran into the powder room carrying a lighted torch. The ship exploded. The oncoming canoes fished up little more

Typical Danish slave ship. Note 3-canvas wind funnels (A private collection, Kobenhavn, Denmark)

Two medals struck from Guinea gold, showing two Danish slaving ships. (National Museum, Denmark)

than 30 Negroes and the ship's boy. The rest, more than 500 slaves, disappeared in the waves.

"Less lucky were the Negroes aboard an English slave ship the same year (1785), also at the Gold Coast. They killed all Europeans, hauled anchor and let the ship drift ashore. When they came into the surf, they jumped overboard and swam ashore. To their distress, soldiers and free-Negroes were waiting for them, took them prisoners, and sold them once again to the Europeans. . . .

"Now, dear Father, let me tell you about the 3rd slave rebellion, the one that I, myself, experienced.

"It was the 2nd day after our departure from the African coast. I was at that time on deck talking with some Akras, since I understood their language. Suddenly I noted that everything had gotten very quiet. Usually there is a lot of noise and commotion aboard. This sudden quiet disturbed me. I proceeded quickly to the rear of the ship to see if the guards were at their posts, particularly the key look-out on the quarterdeck. This is a strategic area where small cannon are mounted. These cannon command a full view of the ship and are fired every evening as a warning to the slaves.

"When I reached about halfway to the quarter-deck, the door was opened by the First Mate, who came out to meet me. At that moment, a cry sounded out from the slaves on deck, the worst cry that one can imagine. I had heard such a cry before. It was a signal for attack, common among the Negroes during battle.

"The slaves closest to me were chained in pairs, the hand of one coupled to the foot of another. Rising suddenly around me, some of them hit me in the head with their hand irons. I fell down among those who had not risen because of the heavy chains on their feet. Since these slaves were so locked that they could hardly move, I crawled away between them and reached for the quarter-deck door. The officers inside wanted to let me in, but they knew if they opened that door the many standing Negroes outside, who were able to maneuver despite their chains, had the power to tear the door apart. It was a case of letting me, one European, be killed rather than permit the Negroes to become master of the door.

The slaves had jumped into the ocean... (Walter Appleton Clark, artist)

The ship's officers tried to fish up as many of the slaves as possible (Walter Appleton Clark, artist)

"The rebelling slaves did not let me stay by the door very long, but forced me down to the floor. Then many hands dragged me by the feet, passing me from one to another, toward the open deck where one slave waited with a knife.

"In a frenzy, he cut me across the forehead, the temples, through my ear and way down in the throat. There he was having trouble plunging the knife in since, very fortunately, I was wearing a thick silk scarf.

"Meanwhile some of the ship's guards had gained control of the lookout station above the quarter-deck and had trained guns on the rebels. At that moment, my salvation came. A bullet, fired from the quarter-deck, penetrated the chest of my would be executioner. He fell backwards. Other hands, holding me down, let go. I was freed. The cannon shots cleared a way to the quarter deck.

"I barely had the strength to crawl towards the quarter-deck door, while a fountain of blood marked my way, since my right temple artery had been sliced through.

"Near the quarter-deck door, I fainted. When I regained consciousness, I found myself on a couch. The captain of the ship, himself, was wetting my head with some hot wine. It all seemed like a bad dream. I tried to stand up, but I could not. My head was heavy as lead. The cloth bandages were soaked with blood.

"Because of the many blows that I had received from the slave irons (one of them had knocked a hole in my head), my wounds were deep and very inflamed. As the muscles of the temple had been cut, my teeth had locked and I could hardly open my mouth. I had to be given liquid foods to sustain me. . . .

". . . Several hours passed before the revolt was brought under control. Those of the Negroes who had not participated in the uprising were sent below deck. The others had jumped into the ocean.

"The ship's officers lowered the boats to try to fish up as many of the slaves as possible. It was surprising how some coupled pairs, having only one arm and one free leg, had managed to keep their heads above water. Some faced death with such stubbornness that they pushed the rescue ropes away and drowned by their own free will. There was a coupled pair, where one

Fort Christianborg and sea approaches, engraving by J. Hill, 1806
(Macpherson Collection, London)

Fort Christianborg with slave huts near by (Danish State Archives,
Kobenhavn, Denmark)

wanted to be rescued, the other one not and the one who wanted to die, forced the other one under.

"By counting, we found that we had lost 34 negroes. Among the Europeans, there was nobody dead, only two wounded.

"About me, even though my condition had looked rather bad, I recovered from my wounds, and the day I arrived in the West Indies, two months after the rebellion, I was healed. If you ask me why the Negroes were so frantic to kill me, I found out later. As I had been the last to board the ship, they believed that I was the principal owner of the slaves. They thought that by sending me into the next world first, it would be a simple matter to get rid of the others.

"Afterwards, during the voyage, they came to like me. In the mornings when I went down to see them and gave them medical care, they received me with a strong clapping of hands, which among these people is a sign of approval just as we do in the theatre.

"Without the unfortunate uprising, we would have had a very lucky voyage, since only seven Negroes died from sickness, a very low percentage when you consider the large number of persons we were carrying. Some ships lose as much as 50 percent of their human cargoes between Africa and the West Indies.

"On our ship the greatest cleanliness was undertaken. Every second day the slaves would come up on deck to get fresh air and exercise. Our canvas air-stacks were so arranged as to catch the maximum amount of wind and send it below. Before the Negroes were sent back down, the holds were thoroughly smoked out.

"We gave them plenty of well cooked porrage, beans, and fresh fish, which we were lucky to catch in abundance especially as we got close to the Equator. . . .

"Shortly after our arrival in St. Croix, the slaves were prepared for sale. They were given extra rations. Limbs and bodies were washed and oiled. Then, in groups, our Negroes were paraded ashore before many spectators.

"The sales-day arrived. Our entire human cargo was transferred to a large auction-house. At a designated moment, a door was flung open. An army of planters stormed in and furiously grabbed Negroes and Negresses they had noticed and visually selected during the previous days. The whole affair happened with such speed and fury that I was startled. One can imagine the fright of the Negroes.

"Before four hours had passed, the greater part of the slaves were sold. Only 48 remained, most of them invalids or old Negroes. They were sold next day for an average of 750 kroner each. The total amount derived from the auction was more than 364,000 kroner.

"The more that one sees of slavery, the more it sickens the spirit of a moral and decent person. One can only have deep pity for the miserable victim of a cruel owner and there are many such owners.

"I saw one poor slave tied to a pole and whipped until it seemed that his flesh was coming apart. And all because of some simple misdemeanor that enraged his master.

"None will treat their slaves more barbarically than the free mulattoes, or those mixes between Europeans and Negroes. Such a female mulatto in my neighborhood owned a slave woman who had broken something by accident. To take revenge on her, the cruel owner tied the hands of her offending slave and hung her up on a spike in the wall. Taking her dress off, this beast of a woman slowly stung her with a needle, all over her body, so that the poor human being was crying out something terrible. The cruel mulatto woman continued this torture for more than an hour, until merciful neighbors came running, begging for the slave woman.

"These cruel owners create the reason for most of the crimes committed by slaves. They demand that Negroes be servile and not run away; but they give them every reason for doing so.

"I always feel saddened to watch these unhappy people being driven to work like cattle. Thirty or 40 of them, with picks on their shoulders, move forward with one or two bombas cracking their whips in the air. If a slave forgets himself for a moment, he right away tastes the lash of the whip.

"I often ask myself when I see these groups of wretched people and the bombas driving them: Oh, poor human beings, what were you before? And what are you now?. . . .

Rain Forest, St. Croix from the Henry Morton Sketchbook 1843–1844
(Courtesy the St. Croix Landmarks Society)

In the letter from St. Croix, D.W.I. (March 12, 1787) to his father in Copenhagen, Isert expressed an idea that was later to dominate his thinking and actions; his deep seated conviction that carrying slaves from Africa to the Western Hemisphere and the West Indies was a great historical blunder, commercial as well as moral:

"Why did our forefathers not have the sense to found plantations right there on the fertile continent of Africa; plantations for sugar, coffee, cacao, cotton and other articles that had become so necessary in Europe?

"Had we gone to Africa with the leaf of the olive tree in our hands rather than weapons of murder, willingly would the natives have given us access to the best and most fertile parts of their lands, areas which for untold years had been lying desolate. Why was not our approach more Christian, more intelligent and humane? Why?

"Those African people would have helped us in freedom, and for low wages would have given us greatness and riches with no offense against nature, or our personal and national consciences.

"Why did we have to uproot vast numbers of people from their homelands, subject them to agony, torture, humiliation, and death; transplant them to alien continents, Caribbean islands, big and small? Why?

"Great plantations could be founded where free Africans would do the work, but under good conditions. At the same time, they would be educated, and the terrible slave trade with all its immoral aspects would not be necessary."

Paul Erdmann Isert spent several weeks in St. Croix. In his letters to his family in Denmark, he described the beauty of the island, its lush rain forests and flowering plants; its good roads, its well organized plantations, and hospitable people.

He found St. Croix almost as hot as Guinea but more pleasant because of the constant trade breezes. He noted that the pearl-hens (Guinea fowl) imported from Africa adapted as well to St. Croix as they did in Guinea.

On a visit to St. Thomas (April, 1787), he described the thriving commerce there:

"All nations are doing business here, with the North

Heinrich Carl von Schimmelmann, father of the count, Lonberg ca. 1773
(Fredericksberg Museum, Denmark)

Count Ernst von Schimmelmann, prominent Danish capitalist, by Erik
Paulsen (Holsteinberg)

Americans most active. They seem to supply the island with most of the basic food stuffs and in return are the island-merchants best customers for European manufactured goods. The traders, here, tell me that the Americans are more prompt in meeting their payments than the Europeans.

"Many local merchants thrive on illegal trade with Porto Rico and islands in the Spanish Main. Payments received are mostly in Spanish dollars, but there is a considerable amount of outright barter.

"From St. Thomas, I continued my voyage and saw several smaller islands: St. John, Tortola, Anegada. Next we saw Saba, St. Martin, and St. Eustatius, the latter looking from the distance like a hay stack. On coming nearer, what seemed like a single cone became two separate hills, the larger towards the east exposing what appeared to be the burnt out crater of an extinct volcano.

"Later, we passed the sugar islands of St. Kitts and Montserrat. Five days sailing from there brought us to the beautiful island of Guadeloupe, where I stayed for almost a month. From Guadeloupe we continued our voyage past the islands of Mariegalante and Dominica and arrived at Martinique, from which island I am now sending you my last letter describing the voyage. Tomorrow we head back to St. Croix and then, if God so wills, we depart for Copenhagen."

Dr. Isert returned to Denmark. With the zeal of an inspired missionary, he expounded his views to every important official of the government who would listen to him.

He told them of his experiences in Africa. He described in detail the horror and agony that he had personally witnessed on the slave ships carrying their human cargoes to the West Indies. He gave them firsthand information of the slave system as it operated in the Danish West Indies. Above all else, he offered his plan to put an end to the evil traffic with a minimum of economic dislocation.

Isert's pleas did not fall on deaf ears. He enlisted the powerful support of Count Ernst Schimmelmann, then Minister of the Treasury for the Danish Government.

A deeply religious and compassionate man, Count Schimmelmann had assumed the leadership of the Danish liberals in

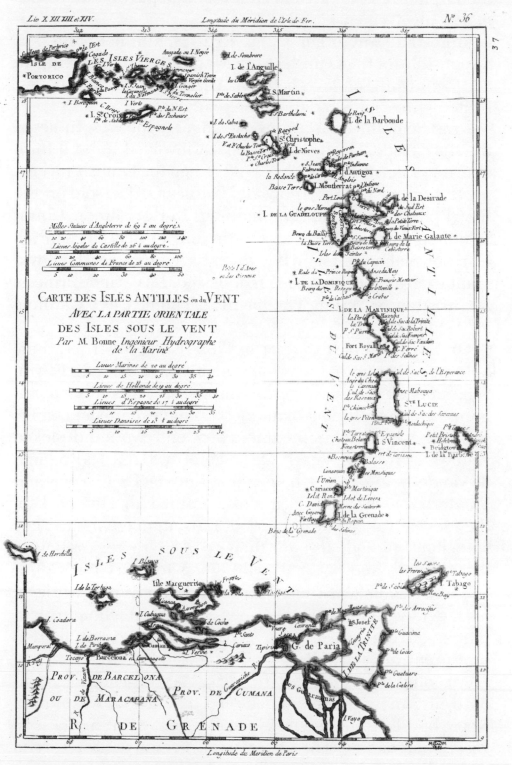

Isert's route down the West Indian island chain..., ca. 1780 (Courtesy
Mapes Monde Co. Ltd., Rome)

their fight to end the system of slavery and particularly Denmark's involvement.

More than any other Dane, Ernst Schimmelmann was responsible for the Danish law of March 10, 1792, putting an end to the traffic of slaves between Africa and the Danish West Indies, with a cut-off date in the year 1803.

Ernst Schimmelmann was no stranger to the West Indies or the slave trade. His family had been involved in both for a quarter of a century. In April 1763, when the Danish government, through its West India and Guinea Office, sold off the Royal plantations and slave holdings in the islands, Count Schimmelmann's father, the wealthy and influential Heinrich Carl von Schimmelmann bought at bargain prices the Royal plantations of La Grange in Frederiksted, La Grande Princess in Christiansted, estate Thomas in St. Thomas, and Caroline in St. John.

On the death of his father in 1782, Ernst inherited these holdings. He sent out his young nephew, H. Ludvig E. von Schimmelmann to manage these properties with orders to administer the plantations in the most humane manner possible.

Later, Count Schimmelmann sent out two hand-picked young men from Denmark, De La Porte and Charles Boudeus de Vanderbourg, to help his nephew, Ludvig. De La Porte and Vanderbourg had been carefully trained in Denmark in the most advanced techniques of farm management. They were hand-picked, also, for their good characters, religious backgrounds and personal willingness to carry out Count Schimmelmann's insistence on humane handling of workers.

Under the guidance of these men, the Schimmelmann plantations, on the island of St. Croix particularly, became models for the entire West Indies.

An enlightened practice that developed and became standard custom for the Schimmelmann plantations was to send Negro boy slaves to Denmark for education, with emphasis on vocational training. These young men, in most cases, returned to the islands and, deeply loyal to their benefactor, took important positions on the plantations. Their fluency with the Danish language gave them special status in the islands.

So it was little wonder that Count Ernst Schimmelmann lent

Artillery Officer, Danish Guinea Fort. (The Danish State Archives, Kobenhavn, Denmark)

a willing ear to the revolutionary ideas of Paul Erdmann Isert, and the more the Count listened to the young doctor, the more convinced he became that Isert's concepts had real merit.

Schimmelmann offered to finance Isert in an initial experiment in Africa to purchase a large and suitable tract of land, to develop a plantation and to use free African labor exclusively.

The Danish historian, Thorkild Hansen, tells us that:

"Count Schimmelmann arranged that on Isert's return to Africa, he would go with substantial authority. He secured for the young man a commission in the Danish army with a title of Captain in the Infantry.

"Isert's official instructions written by Count Schimmelmann himself, on behalf of the King, and co-signed by C.V. Brant, not only show clearly Schimmelmann's respect and admiration for Isert but also the Count's feelings of responsibility towards the Danish State.

"Furthermore, the written instructions showed Schimmelmann's superior understanding of Isert's ideas, as well as Schimmelmann's own deep, warm feelings of pity and compassion for the Negroes as victims of the European nations wild and unlimited selfishness and cruelty. . . .

"During his stay in Denmark," wrote Thorkild Hansen, "Isert married a vicar's daughter, Dorothea Elizabeth Plum. The marriage took place April 3, 1788. The same year, July 10, 1788, Isert received the Royal Appointment, and four days later, he, his wife, and a selected few persons, started the voyage to Guinea. In the middle of November 1788, the ships reached the harbour of Christiansborg. . . .

Note: *The ship's Captain Berg was the same one who had taken Isert from Africa to the Danish West Indies when the slave uprising occurred that almost cost Isert his life. So influenced had Capt. Berg become by the doctrines of Isert, that Berg never again transported slaves from Africa to the West Indies. I.P.*

"Isert and his party stayed at Christiansborg for a few days, and then leaving the safety of the Danish fort, travelled to the outlying district of Malfi which he had considered an ideal place to start his experiment. But he had not figured on the hot and unhealthy climate there, and fearing for the health of

A warrior nobleman of Accra by M. Rosler & C.L. Schmidt (Kobenhavn, mid 18th Century)

his wife and party, he returned to the Danish settlement on the coast...."

While at Christiansborg, Guinea, Dr. Isert was visited by an old friend, Count Attiambo, the powerful leader of an African tribe friendly to the Danes.

During his period of service as chief physician of the Danish hospital at Christiansborg (1783-1785), Isert had done many favors and given frequent medical help to Attiambo and his followers. A warm and close friendship had developed between the two men, and Count Attiambo was overjoyed to see his friend again. The Danish historian, Thorkild Hansen, tells us that:

"Attiambo listened to Isert and became very enthusiastic about his friend's plans for plantation development in which free Africans would play an important role. Right away, Attiambo called together his advisors and explained to them Isert's plans. His Advisory Council came up with the unanimous decision that it would be to the advantage of their country to cooperate with the Danes. They worked out an agreement that Isert should found plantations adjacent to their villages so long as he did not disturb land already in use by the Negroes.

"Attiambo's followers helped Isert to put up a temporary home in the area selected by the Doctor for his experiment. They also helped him to cut a road from this area, through the jungle, and down to the coast. In this initial experiment, Isert planned to plant cotton on the fields between the mountains and the coast.

"On December 21, 1788, Isert and his party moved into their completed quarters and in an elaborate ceremony Attiambo and his board of advisors officially transferred the area to Isert as the representative of the Danish Crown.

"Attiambo himself, and two of his top noblemen, planted the Danish flag at the entrance to the enclave and swore that from that moment, and forever after, they would be true and steadfast friends of Denmark. A formal decree, prepared beforehand by the Danish King was signed by Attiambo and his Council.

"Isert named the colony Frederiksnopel after the then Crown Prince of Denmark. White craftsmen began to build more stonehouses and friendly Negroes, working for wages, cleared the woodland.

"The first seeds sown were for kitchen vegetables, cotton, indigo, and tobacco. Isert had brought with him from Denmark seeds from most of the European garden plants, expecting them to thrive well in the African mountains. He also had brought some domestic animals from Europe.

"From the beginning, everything seemed to develop well. The Negroes were extremely friendly and helpful, and in his initial report to Denmark from Frederiksnopel, Guinea, dated January 1789, Isert wrote warmly and optimistically about the progress that was being made.

"Five days later, Paul Erdmann Isert was dead!

"Earliest reports reaching Denmark from officials in Christiansborg attributed his death to fever. Later reports indicated that Isert had been murdered in a plot by slave traders and conniving settlement officials.

"That Isert was sick seems very unlikely, since in the report dated only five days before his death, Isert was not only filled with optimism, but he had placed large orders for European goods and equipment. There was no lack of strength or inspiration in his report.

"Evidence continued to grow that Isert's initial successes, and what they portended for the future, had so disturbed the slave traders and their official supporters, that they plotted together and killed him.

"Isert's ideas, already beginning to work out in practice by creating an attractive social and economic alternative to slavery for both black and white, clearly represented a massive threat to the lucrative slave trade which its powerful exploiters could not tolerate. So they killed him!

"When Isert died, his ideas fell apart. There was no one with his zeal and missionary spirit to take over.

"Isert's sorrowing wife gave birth to a baby girl one month later, February 18, 1789. The child was named Pauline after her dead father, but the child died a month later from lack of care. Her distraught mother had died seven days after delivery.

"Count Ernst Schimmelmann was very shaken when he received news of the unfortunate happenings at Frederiksnopel.

He had great expectations for Isert's work and now it had come to a violent end.

"In the Danish literary journal, *Minerva*, published in Copenhagen, Bishop Plum, Isert's brother-in-law, expressed his grief in a poem:

Death tore our Isert
Away from us, in the middle
Of his beautiful, honourable life.

The murder-angels of Barbary
With terrible blood-stained wings
So long hovering about Africa
Have killed our noble Isert.

His heart was filled
For Humanity, All Humanity.
He bought land, built a town
With great hopes for Africa's sons.

He saw hope, activity and diligence
Beginning to flower along
The shores of the Volta.

He saw children of the country
Learning to work the soil
Of their own native land
He saw them growing in freedom.

Alas, alas, Death has torn our
Isert away from us, in his prime
In vain, he made a great plan
In Denmark's honour, what courage.

Nobody has the courage, nobody
Like our poor Isert, to do
What he started to do
For the sake of all Humanity.

He put his Life at stake
To administer such a huge task
What desire, what strength
To put his Life at stake for all.

Nobody else is familiar with
The nature, the country, its languages
Like our poor Isert, nobody else
Can walk the road he made.

Now he is gone, his wife and child
All sacrificed in vain, in vain
And all in Denmark's honour
And soon, Denmark will forget him.

"During the period that followed Isert's death," concludes Hansen, "there were several attempts made to carry out his ideas and to found plantations in Africa.

"Unfortunately, these plantations and their great potentials collapsed as soon as their creators died. There was never anyone to take over who had the interest, knowledge, or energy to carry on.

"Nor did anyone have Isert's religious fervor, missionary zeal, or ability to understand and get along with the African people. Isert's untimely death was a monumental disaster."

Sources

1. Westergaard, Waldemar, *The Danish West Indies Under Company Rule, 1671-1754* (New York: 1917).

2. Paul Erdmann Isert, *Reise nach Guinea und den Carabaischen Inseln, in Columbien, in Briefen an seine Freunden beschreiben* (Kjobenhavn: 1788).

3. Paul Erdmann Isert, by Ingeborg Raunkiaer. *Reise til Guinea og ed Caribaeiske Oer. Samling af de bedste og nyeste Reisebeskrivelser*, bind III (Kobenhaven: 1790). *Ny forkortet udg. ved. Ingeborg Raunkiaer* (Kobenhaven: 1917).

4. Hansen Thorkild, *Slavernes Kyst* (Slave Coast) Gylendal (Kobenhaven: 1967). *Slavernes Skibe* (Slave Ships), Gylendal (Kobenhaven: 1968). *Slavernes Oer* (Slave Island), Gylendal (Kobenhaven: 1970).

5. Poem by Bishop Plum, *Minerva* (Kobenhaven: 1789).

III
Horrors of the Middle Passage

The term, *"Middle Passage,"* arose in reference to the voyages of slave-laden vessels from the African coast to slave markets in the Americas.

The voyages lasted from eight to ten weeks and sometimes longer. They occurred in the torrid zone where equatorial heat, drawn out calms, and sudden storms added to the suffering of the slaves. Unbearable conditions, intensified by overcrowding, caused massive elimination of the sick and the weak among the human cargoes.

In his book, *Slave Ships and Slavery*, George Francis Dow tells us: "The cruelty and horror of the *'Middle Passage,'* can never be told in all its gruesome details. It is enough to recall that the ships were always trailed by man-eating sharks."

"Between decks where the slaves were stored," wrote an 18th-century commentator, "there can hardly a man fetch his breath by reason there ariseth such a funk in the night that it causeth putrification of the blood and breedeth disease much like the plague."

A 19th-century observer noted: "Were the Atlantic ocean dried up today, one could trace the pathway between the slave coast of Africa and America by a scattered roadway of human bones."

I.P.

The mortality rate of slave cargoes was directly related to the care and cleanliness of quarters in which the bulk of the slaves were stored. So the proper stowage of slaves, particularly at night, was of vital importance to a successful crossing from the Guinea Coast to the West Indies and America.

On a well run slave ship, the process of stowing the slaves for the night began at sundown. One of the best descriptions of the process is to be found in the account of Capt. Theodore Canot as told to Brantz Mayer:

"The second mate and boatswain descend into the hold, whip in hand, and range the slaves in their regular places; those on the right side of the vessel facing forward and lying in each other's laps, while those on the left are similarly stowed with their faces towards the stern. In this way each Negro lies on his right side, which is considered preferable for the action of the heart.

"In allotting places, particular attention is paid to size, the taller being selected for the greatest breath of the vessel, while the shorter and younger are lodged near the bows."

The Danes always claimed that organization and treatment aboard the Danish ships were better than on the British ones. Treatment on the latter was supposed to be the worst possible, not only because of the tendency of the British to overcrowd their ships but because of the notorious brutality of the British captains, officers and crews.

The end result, mortality-wise, depended almost entirely on the organization and management aboard individual slave ships regardless of which national flag was flown. Statistics in the Danish State Archives demonstrate this clearly. There are extremes represented by the Danish slaver *Acras* with a death percentage of 43.3 percent, while the Danish slaver *Ada* reported less than 1 percent.

Close to the end of the monopoly period of the Danish West India and Guinea Company, precise records were kept of the movement of slaves to St. Croix on Danish vessels. The total was 6513. The death rate was 1056.

On slave ships that were poorly organized and overcrowded, negroes were jammed into the holds with little regard for stowage. "They were literally piled one on top of another and

Method of stowing slaves in limited space aboard slave ships (Clarkson's *Abolition of the Slave Trade*, London, 1808) the unsteady motion of the ship, combined with foul air and great heat made the place simply horrible...."

Invariably, epidemics broke out under such conditions. According to the British ship doctor, Alexander Falconbridge:

"When the sea was rough and the rain heavy, it became necessary to close the air vents. Fresh air being thus excluded, the Negroes' storage area grew intolerably hot. The confined air, rendered noxious by the effuvia exhaled from their bodies and by being repeatedly breathed, soon produced fevers and fluxes which generally carried off great numbers of them....

"Frequently, I went down among them till the hold became so unbearably hot that I could not stay. Excessive heat was not the only thing that rendered the situation intolerable. The floor of the hold was so covered with blood and mucus which proceeded from them in consequence of the flux, that it resembled a slaughter house.

"It is not in the power of the human imagination to picture a situation more dreadful or disgusting. Numbers of the slaves having fainted, they were carried on deck where several of them died and the rest, with great difficulty, were restored....

"Upon going down in the mornings to examine the condition of the slaves, I frequently found several dead, and among the men, sometimes a dead and living Negro fastened by their irons together. When this was the case, they were brought upon the deck and laid on the grating when the living Negro was disengaged and the dead one thrown overboard.

"An exertion of the greatest skill and attention could afford the diseased Negroes little relief so long as the causes of the diseases, namely, the breathing of a putrid atmosphere and wallowing in their own excrements, remain. When once the fever and flux get to any height at sea, a cure is scarcely ever effected...."

Note: *"flux" is the early name for amoebic dysentery, an ulcerative inflammation of the colon. It may reach the liver by the portal blood stream, producing abcesses on that organ. Today we know that this acute form of dysentery is caused not by "foul air" and "excessive heat" but by the organism Entamoeba histolytica found in bad water and rotted food. I.P.*

"By constantly lying in the blood and mucus flowing from those afflicted with the flux, others contracted it," continued Falconbridge. "Few were able to withstand the fatal effects of it. The utmost skill of the surgeon was here ineffectual."

From the very beginning of the slave movement from Africa to the West Indies and America, mention is made of the ruinous effects of the flux on slave cargoes and ships' crews. Whether it be the 16th, 17th, 18th, or 19th centuries, the record is there showing a constant dread of the flux and its devastating effects.

Sir John Hawkins, the great sea captain and first Englishman to engage in the slave trade between the Guinea Coast and America in the year 1563, limited the number of his crew "for fear of the flux and other inconveniences whereunto men in long voyages are commonly subjected to...."

Another quote, typical of the 18th century, taken from a narrative: *The Journal of Capt. Thomas Phillips* (printed in London, 1764) declared:

"This distemper which my men as well as the blacks mostly died of, was the white flux, which was so violent and inveterate that no medicine would in the least check it; so that when any of our men were seized by it, we esteemed him a dead man, as he generally proved...."

So severely were Negroes afflicted with the flux at times, declared Falconbridge, that he had seen many of them, after being landed, obliged by the pain and virulence of the complaint to stop almost every minute to seek relief.

Falconbridge described in detail one of the deceptions practiced by a ship's captain:

"A Liverpool captain boasted of his having cheated some Jews by the following stratagem: A lot of slaves afflicted with the flux being landed for sale, he directed his ship's surgeon to stop the extremity of each of them with oakum. Thus prepared, they were taken to the place of sale, where being unable to stand but for a very short time, they were permitted to sit.

"The Jews, when they examined them, obliged them to stand in order to see if there be any discharge, and when there was no appearance of such, they considered it a symptom of recovery. A bargain was struck and the slaves were bought. But it was not long before discovery of the cheat followed, for the

Slaves crowded aboard and the force feeding of a slave

excruciating pain which the prevention of the discharge occasioned, could hardly be borne by the sick ones. The obstructions were removed and the deluded buyers were speedily convinced of the imposition. . . ."

Falconbridge did not mention if this incident occurred in St. Thomas, but it is most probable that it did.

The records of the period tell us that a group of Jews and surgeons conducted a "rehabilitation" farm on the eastern end of St. Thomas to which they carried many of these desperately sick slaves. After intensive care with the help of experienced "bush doctors" as well as full utilization of medical knowledge available at the time, they effected a considerable number of remarkable recoveries.

Journals of slave ship captains and doctors from the 18th and early 19th centuries show marked agreement in one area. Of all calamities that might occur on the passage from Africa to the West Indies and America, the calamity most dreaded was an outbreak of smallpox.

So unmanageable and so catastrophic were the effects of this virulent disease that every well organized slaver carried preventative medicine on board in the form of potent poisons.

Ship captains, doctors, and experienced staff men did not hesitate at the first sign of the disease to try to isolate and destroy the affected person or persons. Acting quickly and desperately, they hoped to stop the spread of the deadly pox to the rest of the ship.

In the *Adventures of an African Slaver*, Capt. Theodore Canot vividly describes two such experiences, the first aboard the slave ship *San Pablo*:

"We had been several days buffeting a series of adverse gales when word was brought to me after a night of weary watching, that several slaves were ill of small pox. The news appalled me. I called the officers into my cabin for consultation.

"The gales had lasted nine days and with such violence that it was impossible to take off the gratings, release the slaves, purify the decks, or rig the wind-sails. When the first lull occurred, a thorough inspection of the 800 slaves had been made, and a death announced. As life had departed during the tempest, a careful inspection of the body was made, and it was this that first disclosed the pestilence in our midst. The corpse was silently thrown into the sea, and the malady kept secret from crew and Negroes.

"When breakfast was over on that fatal morning, I determined to visit the slave deck myself, and ordering an abundant supply of lanterns, descended to the cavern, which still reeked horribly with the human vapor, even after ventilation. Here I found nine of the Negroes infected by the disease.

"We took counsel as to the use of laudanum in ridding ourselves speedily of the sufferers—a remedy that is used secretly in desperate cases to preserve the living from contagion. It was quickly resolved that the disease had already gone too far, when nine were prostrated, to save the rest by depriving the nine of life. Accordingly, these wretched beings were at once sent to the forecastle as a hospital.

"The ship's hold was then ventilated and limed, yet before the gale abated, our sick list was increased to 30. The hospital could hold no more. Twelve of the sailors took infection and 15 corpses had been cast into the sea. All reserve was now at an end. Body after body fed the deep.

"When the wind and waves had lulled so much as to allow the gratings to be removed from our hatches, our consternation knew no bounds when we found that nearly all the slaves were dead or dying.

There was no time for languor. Twelve of the stoutest survivors were ordered to drag out the dead from among the ill, and though the twelve were constantly drenched with rum to brutalize them, still we were forced to aid the gang by reckless volunteers from our crew, who, arming their hands with tarred mittens, flung the foetid masses of putrefaction into the sea.

"At length death was satisfied, but not until the 800 beings we had shipped in high health had dwindled to 497 skeletons. . . ."

In the other instance, Capt. Canot described how quick and desperate action aboard the slaver *La Estrella* stopped an epidemic from spreading:

"We made land at Porto Rico and were swiftly passing its beautiful shores, when the inspector called my attention to the appearance of one of our attendant slaves, whom he had drilled

The corpse was silently thrown into the sea… (Walter Appleton Clark, artist)

as a sort of cabin boy. He was a gentle, intelligent child and had won the hearts of all the officers.

"His pulse was high, quick and hard; his face and eyes, red and swollen. On his neck I detected half a dozen rosy pimples. He was sent immediately to the forecastle, free from contact with anyone else and left there, cut off from the crew till I could guard against pestilence. It was smallpox!

"The boy passed a wretched night of fever and pain, developing the malady with all its horrors. It was likely that I slept as badly as the sufferer, for my mind was busy with his doom. Daylight found me on deck in consultation with our veteran boatswain, whose experience in the trade authorized the highest respect for his opinion. Hardened as he was, the old man's voice was husky as he whispered the verdict in my ear. I guessed it before he said a word. As we went aft to the quarterdeck, all eyes were bent on us, for everyone conjectured the malady and feared the result, yet none dared ask a question.

"I ordered a general inspection of the slaves, yet when a favourable report was made, I did not rest content, and descended to examine each one personally. It was true, the child alone was infected.

"For half an hour, I trod the deck to and fro restlessly, and caused the crew to subject themselves to inspection. But my sailors were as healthy as the slaves. There was no symptom that indicated approaching danger. I was disappointed again. A single case — a single sign of peril in any quarter — would have spared the poison.

"That evening, in the stillness of the night, a trembling hand stole forward to the afflicted boy with a potion that knows no waking. In a few hours, all was over, life and the pestilence were crushed together. . . ."

Narrative after narrative record the scourge of smallpox aboard the slavers. Time and again the horror repeated itself. In the *Revelations of a Slave Smuggler,* Capt. Richard Drake, an African trader for 50 years (1807-1857), describes a smallpox epidemic aboard the slave ship *Boa Morte,* Capt. Pierre Le clerc:

"The captain's illness turned out to be smallpox and two of the crew soon came down with it. It was impossible to

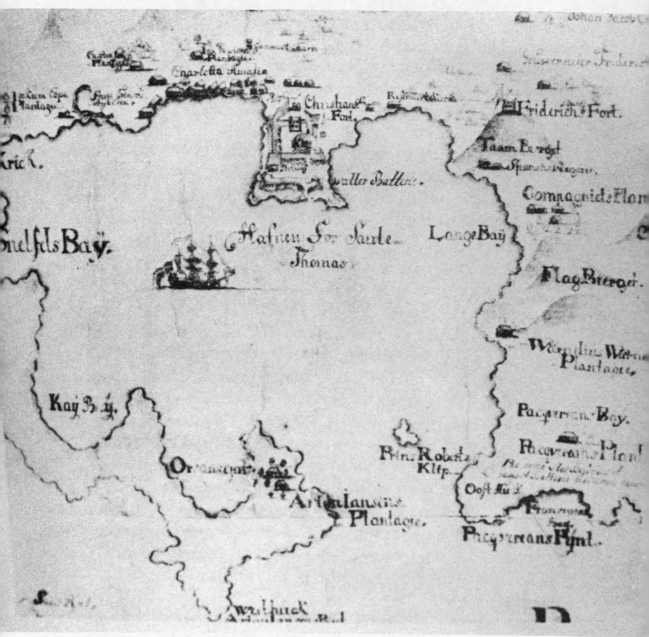

Map of St. Thomas harbor and surroundings, 1730 (Danish National
Archives Kobenhavn, Denmark)

keep the disease from the slaves and the ship turned out to be well named.

"We soon began to feed corpses to the sharks and one day hauled 60 bodies out of the hold. The crew revolted at this work and we had to rely on gangs of slaves to drag the dead heaps from among the living."

Sharks followed the slave ships from the time they left the African coast. Whether attracted by the pungent smell of the "slaver" or the daily ration of bodies that were thrown overboard, the records of the time repeatedly note the presence of these scavengers.

The voyage took weeks, even months, until the vessel finally arrived at its destination. Sometimes Fate intervened to add horror and destruction to human misery. In his diary covering the year 1793, Johan Nissen tells of two overcrowded slave ships finally reaching the entrance of St. Thomas's harbour only to be destroyed by a dreadful hurricane in which all lives were lost, officers, crewmen, and the entire cargo of slaves.

Sources

1. For precise statistics on the movement of slaves from Africa to the Danish West Indies, see Records of the Danish West Indies and Guinea Company, Danish State Archives (Copenhagen, Denmark).

2. Alexander Falconbridge, *Account of the Slave Trade on the Coast of Guinea* (London: 1788).

3. Thomas Phillips, *Journal of Capt. Thomas Phillips* (London: 1764). A description of his experiences with the slave trade, late 17th century. Phillips commanded the English slave ship, *Hannibal*.

4. For a description of the British Slave Trade see, Clarkson, *Abolition of the Slave Trade* (London: 1808). He describes the horrors, brutality and overcrowding that occurred under the British flag at the height of the slave trade.

5. Capt. Richard Drake, *Revelations of a Slave Smuggler* 1807-1857 (New York: 1860). Being the Autobiography of Capt. Drake, an African Trader for fifty years.

6. Capt. Theodore Canot, *Twenty Years of an African Slaver* (New York: 1854).

7. George Francis Dow, *Slave Ships and Slaving* (Salem Massachusetts: 1927).

8. Johan Peter Nissen, *Annual Recordings of Events in and Around St. Thomas, 1792-1837* (Senseman & Company Nazareth, Pennsylvania: 1838).

IV
Murder Trial
of Capt. James De Wolfe

While researching early colonial documents at The New-York Historical Society, this writer came upon a handwritten manuscript dealing with the "Trial for Murder of Capt. James De Wolfe at the Courthouse in St. Thomas, Danish West Indies, April 16, 1795."

The manuscript is included in a collection of letters, public documents, and speeches of colonial statesman, Rufus King (1755-1827).

After a brilliant career in politics, Rufus King was named Ambassador to Great Britain (1796-1803) by George Washington.

During the early 1790's, Rufus King was a member of an inner circle of close friends and trusted advisers surrounding George Washington. Also in this group was William Bradford, Governor of Rhode Island and father-in-law of Capt. James De Wolfe.

Somehow, Rufus King received and put into his file a copy of the "Trial for Murder of Capt. James De Wolfe at the Courthouse in St. Thomas, Danish West Indies, April 16, 1795."

The Rufus King papers were donated to The New-York Historical Society, May 6, 1902, by Mrs. Charles R. King, in accordance with the wishes of her late husband, Dr. Charles R. King, third generation descendant of Rufus King.

I.P.

Ap. 29.95 (26)

Bernt Christian Stevensen his Royal Majesty's of Denmark, Judge and recorder of the Island of St Thomas in America, make known that in the year 1795 the 17th of April at 10 o'Clock in the fore-noon, there was held a Police Court at St Thomas in the house N° 6 Kings Ward and the Court attended by Bernt Christian Stevensen his Royal Majesty's of Denmark Judge and Recorder of the Island of St Thomas in America; in the presence of the Men Gran & Dahr. when in consequence of Auditor Petri's memorial of yesterday's date, a Police examination took place. Auditor Petri, met and presented the notification given, together with the Colonels order for this Court, he then presented his questions agreeable to which he begged the Witness examined. ——

The presented order is as follows — Memorial —
The given in complaint from one Isaac Manchester. I have received — As this Complaint speaks of so great a piece of Cruelty that I consistent with the duties of my Office can by no means omit making known to your Excellency; that the Criminal according to his deserts may be reprimanded and punished — Yr most Obedt Servt Petri ——
Col & Commandant de Malleville ——

Laid before a Police Court at St Thomas 17 April 1795 —
Brown, Constable and Police Master .. You will please to examine the Complaint of Isaac Manchester, against Capt James de Wolfe, which with this is returned immediately and if the same should be lawfully be proved true, and of that nature, that personal confinement for further Punishment, according to Law, may be found necessary, to have recourse thereto immediately — After which when I receive your report on the subject, shall issue the necessary Orders, for commencing a suit against said De Wolfe. St Thomas 16. April 1795
J de Malleville — Auditor and Kings Attorney Petri —
Laid before the Police Court at St Thomas 17. April 1795. Brown Constable, and Police Master. The presented notification runs thus —
In consequence of an Order from Lt Coul. & Commandant, de Malleville there must be at ten o'Clock to morrow an extra Court, held over James DeWolfe on the subject of a crime committed by him, at the afternoon Court. They may be called in as Plaintiff, Isaac Manchester, and as Witness Hersey Bidford, together with the complained of Capt James DeWolfe. St Thomas 16 April. Yr mo Obt Servt Petri ——
Stevenson — his Royal Majesty's of Denmark &c —
The aforementioned Persons, have we, through Mr Dance warned to the appointed time and place. so help us God and his holy word
Fran — Russmann —
Laid before the Police Court April 17th 1795 at St Thomas .. Brown Judge — during Stevenson's sickness — The presented questions run as follows —
Questions — In the cause of the Kings Attorney against J DWolf
1 What is the Deponents name, Calling & Religion ?..

Excerpt from the James De Wolfe manuscript.... The Rufus King papers. (Courtesy of The New-York Historical Society)

On the 16th of April, 1795, Christian Frederick Petri, Judge Advocate over the troops of his Danish Majesty, St. Thomas and St. John, and Advocatus Regus, submitted a memorial to the then Commandant of the islands, Thomas von Malleville. The memorial stated that Petri had received a complaint from one Isaac Manchester against Capt. James De Wolfe, a Danish burgher, presently residing in St. Thomas.

So serious was the complaint, declared Petri, that "consistent with the duties of my office, I can by no means omit making it known to your Excellency so that De Wolfe, if guilty, may be reprimanded and punished. . . ." On the same day, Petri received a reply from von Malleville ordering him, based on the complaint of Isaac Manchester, to proceed against Capt. De Wolfe at once.

The case was heard in the Police Court of St. Thomas the very next day, April 17, 1795. Because of the illness of Bent Christian Stenersen, His Royal Majesty's Judge and Recorder for the islands of St. Thomas-St. John, Constable and Police Master Brown took charge of the examination.

Judge Advocate Petri sat in a special observer's chair. Nearby, a group of respected and carefully selected merchants occupied the advisers' box. Isaac Manchester appeared as plaintiff. Capt. James De Wolfe as defendant. Appearing as witness was one Henry Bradford, Danish burgher and captain of a Danish brig then anchored in the harbour of St. Thomas.

Isaac Manchester was called to the stand and after being duly sworn, was asked to state his complaint. Manchester's complaint was as follows:

"Please your Honor, I find it necessary to acquaint you that Capt. James De Wolfe, some time ago, on a voyage from the Danish settlements in Africa to the West Indies threw overboard a Negro woman, alive.

"I hope that you will bring him to a proper account for acting so much against my feelings and the feelings of every good Christian. I never knew of a more inhuman piece of work, and it would be a shame not to punish him for it. . . ."

Isaac Manchester was then asked the following questions: (1) Does the witness know Capt. James De Wolfe? (2) Does the witness know if Capt. James De Wolfe on a passage from the coast of Guinea to the West Indies voluntarily suffered a Negro woman to be thrown overboard who was then *alive*? (3) Can the witness say what induced Capt. De Wolfe to deal thus with said Negro woman?

Manchester replied "that he knew the defendant, James De Wolfe, that he, Manchester, was not on board the ship *Polly* when the incident took place. He among others had heard of it, among which is present here in Court, Capt. H. Bradford."

Manchester had heard many others speak of it, even in North America. This had induced him to bring in his complaint here in St. Thomas since De Wolfe was a Danish burgher resident in the island. He hoped that De Wolfe might be punished according to his deserts.

Isaac Manchester was thereupon dismissed. Capt. Henry Bradford was called to the stand and sworn in. Capt. Bradford declared that he knew Capt. De Wolfe and was on board De Wolfe's ship *Polly* under the American flag, as a sailor, when the incident took place which the plaintiff had set forth.

The witness declared that he was not on deck when the Negro woman, spoken of, was thrown overboard. He had heard some members of the crew say she was dead and others that she was not. The evening prior to the incident, he, Bradford, had attended a consultation of captain, officers and crew.

What should be done with the Negro woman that was strongly attacked with the smallpox for which she was put in the foretop for fear that she should infect the crew of which three quarters of them had not had it?

Before the consultation was concluded, a sailor was sent into the top who found her greatly swollen upon which it was concluded that the next morning she should be thrown overboard for the aforementioned reasons, whether dead or alive. The ship council did not believe that she could possibly recover as she was so much swelled.

It was felt that it was not possible to keep this Negro woman longer in the foretop without infecting the whole Crew as the top was so near the deck and directly over the place of the sailors' resort. . . . Having no further evidence to give, Capt. Bradford was thanked by the court and dismissed.

Capt. James De Wolfe was called to the stand and duly

Thomas von Malleville (1739–1798), Commandant of the Danish West
India islands in the year 1795 when James De Wolfe was tried (Private
collection of the Kuud Norgaard family, Kobenhavn)

Police Court, Fort Christian, at the time of the trial of Capt. James De Wolfe, 1795. (Private collection of the author, St. Thomas, V.I.)

sworn. He was asked if he had heard the complaint. De Wolfe replied that he had. He was asked if he wished to make a statement to which the defendant replied that he did. He was ordered to proceed.

Capt. De Wolfe declared that in the year 1788, he commanded the ship *Polly*. At the Danish settlement on the coast of Africa he took on board a cargo of 142 Negroes to bring them to the West Indies. It happened on the voyage that a Negro woman got the smallpox.

De Wolfe declared that he had made every effort in his power to help the sick woman. In the beginning he strove to furnish her with all the necessary medicines which he had on hand. When she grew worse, he was afraid the disease would spread itself among the other Negroes and the crew which consisted of 15 men of whom ten had not had the smallpox.

Consequently, with the consent of the ship's officers and men, a conclusion was reached to sacrifice the life of one person than that more for the sake of that one should lose their lives. De Wolfe declared that at the time of consultation with officers and men, some said the Negro woman was dead, others, that she was not, which of the two was the case, the defendant did not know.

De Wolfe declared that immediately on his arrival at the Dutch island of St. Eustatius he had appeared before his Excellency Governor Johannes Runnels and had reported the incident in detail. Furthermore that he, De Wolfe, had in his possession two depositions of witnesses to the incident which had been duly sworn to before the Dutch governor.

De Wolfe requested that these two depositions be read before the Court and be placed in evidence. The court ordered that the two depositions be read and thereafter placed in evidence. The contents of the depositions were revealed as follows:

"Before his Excellency Johannes Runnels, Governor of the island of St. Eustatius and its dependencies, Colonel of the Militia and President of the College, personally appeared Isaac Stockman and Henry Clanning.

"Mariners, being duly sworn upon the Evangelists of Almighty God severally depose and say that they are both natives of Newport in the State of Rhode Island; that they sailed

Polly (Capt. James De Wolfe), taking on cargo of slaves at the Danish settlement, Guinea Coast (Jens-Peter Kemmler, artist)

from one of the Danish settlements on the coast of Africa on or about the 15th day of September 1788, in the ship *Polly* belonging to the said town of Newport in the State of Rhode Island, commanded by Capt. James De Wolfe, with a cargo of slaves.

"About 10 days after their departure from the coast of Africa, the smallpox made its appearance in an alarming manner upon one of the female slaves. In order to prevent this violent disorder from spreading and infecting the ship's crew which consisted of 15 white people (only 5 of which had had it) the diseased woman was carried to the Main Top, where every attention was paid to her and every assistance afforded that the situation they were in, would allow.

"In the course of three or four days, her disorder increased so as to become offensive and to render it dangerous for her to remain on board. In the latitude 2 North, or thereabouts, Capt. De Wolfe, being very much alarmed and under great apprehension, called the mate and the crew together in order to consult with them upon the steps to be taken to prevent this dreadful disorder from getting amongst the crew and cargo.

"Capt. De Wolfe represented to them that it would be, in all probability, at least 50 or 60 days before they could arrive at the port of their destination; that he had it not in his power to afford any effective medical assistance to such as might take the disorder. If it should spread among the crew and cargo, the Negroes must be confined in the hold where the excessive heat would increase the effects of the disease and a dreadful mortality must inevitably ensue.

"To complete this unfortunate situation, the slaves they had on board were of a nation famed for its valour and inclination to revolt. If the crew were attacked with this disease, it would afford the slaves an opportunity to execute any plot they might form.

"Many of the crew were under apprehension for their own personal safety. Were the illness to strike them, they would become incapable of affording any assistance in navigating the vessel, much less of making resistance to a revolt should it be attempted.

"Under these circumstances, and as the severity of the disorder left no appearance of the woman recovering but on

Capt. James De Wolfe (1764–1837)

the contrary confirmed the beliefs of those who had had the smallpox, that she would die in a short time, no alternative was left to save the crew and cargo which consisted of 142 souls, but to throw this one so dangerously infected overboard.

Accordingly, this was done and each of the crew who had had this disorder, together with the captain, joined their assistance in effecting it.

"The said Isaac Stockman and Henry Clanning, do further under oath declare that this act was far from being accompanied with malice or wantonness or for want of due consideration.

"The said Isaac Stockman and Henry Clanning do further solemnly declare that the following deposition has been deliberately read over to them and that they have deposed thereto and subscribed the same without any fee, or reward, or without any fear, dread or compulsory of or from any person what-so-ever, but of their own free will and accord and the same contains the truth, the whole truth and nothing but the truth. . . . "

On the 29th of April 1795, Judge Advocate Christian Frederick Petri handed down his decision

"The cruelty and wanton barbarity of this act in Capt. De Wolfe appeared to me of such a heinous and atrocious nature, so degrading to humanity and called so loud for vengence, I looked upon it as my duty, as a human man and Ex Oficio to call said James De Wolfe to a condign punishment.

"But after having examined the affair in its true light, and heard the depositions of the aforementioned Henry Bradford, Isaac Stockman and Henry Clanning, it appears that this act of James De Wolfe was morally evil, but at the same time physically good and beneficial to a number of beings.

"When considered that this wench in question was infected by the smallpox, the nature of which is known to be so dreadful and dangerous on shore, how much more so on a vessel in the ocean at a great distance from any port and in a latitude where frequent calms add to the intolerable heat which is known to increase the case and facilitate the contagionness of that distemper.

"That said wench had it in the highest and most alarming

Bristol Harbor, Rhode Island, late 18th Century

degree so as not to afford any hope of her recovery, but on the contrary gave room to dread the infection spreading to the crew and cargo which to prevent was Capt. De Wolfe's duty.

"That every man according to Divine laws and the laws of nature has a right to do as much as lays in his power to divert from him and to escape all descending dangers as it is likewise his duty to choose out of two evils the least.

"And lastly that said James De Wolfe did not act in this case merely by his own will, but after a mature deliberation with his officers and crew who found it to be the only means to save them all from misery and destruction.

"In consequence of which circumstances and after having been tried by a jury of respectable merchants, Capt. James De Wolfe, in conformity with the Danish laws and the dictates of nature, is cleared from all accusation and punishment and Isaac Manchester's accusation against him removed and groundless.

Given under my
hand and seal.
St. Thomas,
29th. April 1795
Christian Frederick Petri"

Who was this man, Capt. James De Wolfe, who was tried for murder and acquitted in a St. Thomas courtroom in the year 1795?

Research at the National Archives, Washington, the Rhode Island Historical Society, and the De Wolfe family papers reveal him to have been a most colorful and historic character.

Born in Bristol County, Rhode Island, March 18, 1764, James was the seventh son of Mark Anthony De Wolfe and Abigail Potter. The father, Mark, a native of Guadeloupe, French West Indies, came to Bristol in 1744, met Abigail Potter and married her. They were both eighteen. Between them they produced 15 children, eight boys and seven girls. Four daughters and five sons survived.

James was to become an outstanding member of this remarkable clan that dominated the seaport town of Bristol for several generations.

Records in the National Archives tell us that he went to sea at the age of fifteen. It was during the period of the American Revolutionary War, and the sea was infested with privateers of many nations. His ship was captured by the British off Bermuda and James was imprisoned. He escaped, and they caught him again. As a result of experiencing much cruelty and hardship: "he became a man of force and indomitable energy with no nice ethical distinctions. . . ."

After his release from prison, he went back to his life at sea with growing success. At the age of 26, he owned his own vessel, *The Little Watt.* That year, 1790, he married Nancy Bradford, daughter of Governor William Bradford of Rhode Island, an intimate friend of George Washington.

James's father, Mark Anthony De Wolfe and his uncle, Simeon Potter, were seafaring men who had been active for years in slave trading on the West Coast of Africa. James learned his trade from them.

In partnership with his four brothers, and with the help of their uncle, Simeon Potter, James fitted ships for Africa and the slave trade and sold their human freight in Havana, Cuba, where the De Wolfe brothers developed large plantation holdings. They also traded with other islands of the West Indies, including St. Thomas.

James De Wolfe's earliest voyages as a sea captain were made to the coast of Guinea where he traded for slaves. Rhode Island merchants of highest commercial and social standings backed him. Apparently he had no qualms of conscience and often went to southern ports to personally supervise the sale of his cargoes.

According to George Howe, the Rhode Island historian, the profits were enormous. Quote: "The operation of the De Wolfe brothers' partnership was almost foolproof. Molasses from the De Wolfe plantations in Cuba reached Bristol in De Wolfe vessels, was turned into Rum at the De Wolfe distillery there, and exported with other trade goods again in De Wolfe ships to the Slave Coast of Africa. There the cargoes were exchanged for slaves, and the human freight brought back for sale at the starting point in Cuba.

"Capt. James's distillery on Thames Street, Bristol, converted 300 gallons of molasses every day into 250 gallons of rum. The cost of distillation was 10 cents a gallon. He paid the U.S. Treasury an import duty of 5 cents on every gallon of molasses but received a rebate of 3 cents, called a drawback, when he exported it as rum. . . . " Before he was thirty, Capt. James De Wolfe had "accumulated wealth enough to make him independent for the rest of his life. . . ."

George Howe, a modern-day descendant of the De Wolfe family, tells us: "In 1791, the Federal Grand Jury, in its first session for Rhode Island, returned an indictment of murder against James De Wolfe for jettisoning a female slave who had caught the smallpox on the Middle Passage aboard a bark of which he was master."

The faded indictment, still buried in the files of the U.S. Department of Justice charges that: "James De Wolfe, not having the fear of God before his eyes, but being moved and seduced by the instigation of the Devil . . . did feloniously, willfully and of his malice aforethought, with his hands seized upon the body of said Negro woman . . . and did push, cast and throw her from said vessel unto the Sea and waters of the Ocean, whereby and whereupon she then and there instantly sank, drowned and died. . . ."

George Washington, who was then President, thru his Attorney General John Jay, "issued a capias for Capt. James's arrest, and though Bristol is almost within sight of Newport, the Federal marshal, for the next four years, reported semi-annually to the Court that 'he, James De Wolfe could not be found by me'. In 1795, a more lenient attorney nol-prossed the case. . . ."

Note: *From 1791-1795, the years that Capt. De Wolfe was reported missing, he was a Danish burgher of St. Thomas and had established residence on this island. The evidence indicates that Isaac Manchester, the sea captain who brought charges against De Wolfe in St. Thomas, might well have been the "citizen" who brought charges against De Wolfe in Rhode Island. It is known that Isaac Manchester was a rival sea captain who lived in Bristol and who also traded for slaves on the coast of Africa.*

I.P.

Barkentine *General Jackson* used by James De Wolfe in trade and whale fishery

After his acquittal for murder in St. Thomas, Capt. James De Wolfe returned to Bristol. *The Dictionary of American Biography* tells us something about his last years:

"Some of his vessels entered the fur trade of the Northwest, then whale fishing and finally even went to China. His principal trade, however, continued in the West Indies and when, in 1804, South Carolina threw open her ports to the importation of slaves because of a threatened national prohibition, De Wolfe leaped to aid and ten of the 202 vessels that entered Charleston between 1804 and 1808 belonged to him.

"The attitude of England during the Napoleonic Wars greatly angered and embarrassed De Wolfe and he sustained heavy losses thru the impressment of seamen. He was a strong advocate of war with England and 11 days after the declaration of the War of 1812, he offered the U.S. government, at his own expense, an armed brig of 160 tons, mounting 18 guns and carrying 120 men, called the *Yankee*.

The *Yankee* was immensely successful. It made six cruises in less than three years and captured more than five million dollars' worth of British property.

"After the close of the war, De Wolfe sensed the coming development of manufacturing in the United States. Gradually he withdrew his capital from shipping. He had already built one of the earliest cotton mills in the U.S. at Coventry, Rhode Island, in 1812.

"He sensed, too, that the new industry needed political influence. For 30 years he represented the town of Bristol in the Rhode Island legislature becoming finally Speaker of the House. In 1821, he was elected to the United States Senate. Here he was a strong advocate of protection for the new young industries and he opposed the extension of slavery to Missouri and the West.

"His interest now was no longer in the African slave but in the white mill laborer. He did not like the atmosphere of Washington and resigned his seat in the Senate in 1825 and returned to the legislature of Rhode Island.

"He made the town of Bristol his especial care. Here on a great estate of 1,000 acres, he built himself a stately mansion,

Brigantine *Macdonough*, 300 tons, built for James De Wolfe in 1814 by Caleb Carr

and devised many schemes for the advancement of the town and its industries.

"De Wolfe was tall and commanding in person and very careful about his dress. He died in New York City in 1837...."

George Howe, the family historian, described him as the "handsomest of the five brothers, with florid cheeks, a blunt nose, gray eyes, an upper lip as sheer as a carpenter's plane, and big capable sailor's hands."

It might be appropriate to close the record of this colorful man and his historic connection with St. Thomas on this note. More than 15 years ago, while cleaning a backroom of A.H. Riise's Apothecary, I came across a square and solidly built stone masonary base with a white marble top. From way back in the 19th century, Riise's chemists had used this facility on which to mix medicine. The apothecary had been established in the year 1838.

Since the top marble slab was in excellent condition, we removed it carefully. It was large and very heavy. It took several persons to lift it off and turn it. It proved to be a tombstone: *To the memory of Capt. James De Wolfe who died in New York City, 1837.*

Townhouse of Capt. James De Wolfe, Bristol, Rhode Island (Courtesy Bob Rulan Miller, Rulan-Miller books, St. Thomas V.I. USA)

Sources

1. Trial for Murder of Capt. James De Wolfe at the Courthouse in St. Thomas, Danish West Indies, April 16, 1795, Rufus King Papers, The New York Historical Society.

2. John De Wolfe, *Voyage to the North Pacific*, References to St. Thomas DWI and James De Wolfe, Pages 8, 10 (Bristol, Rhode Island: 1983).

3. Reverend Calbraith B. Perry, *The De Wolfe Book* (Bristol, Rhode Island: 1900). A genealogy of the De Wolfe family compiled in 1900 by Rev. Calbraith B. Perry, a great grandson of Capt. James De Wolfe. Privately printed and paid for by Mrs. Theodore G. De Wolfe Colt.

4. W.H. Munro, *History of Bristol* (Providence: 1880).

5. W.H. Munro, *Tales of an Old Sea Port, Bristol, Rhode Island* (Princeton: 1917).

6. George Howe, *Mount Hope, Bristol, Rhode Island* (New York: 1959).

V

Voyage of the French Slaver, *Le Rodeur*
Opthalmia and Blindness

The story of the French slaver, *Le Rodeur*, and its blind human cargo (1819), first came to this writer's attention in a volume entitled, *The American Slave Trade*, by John R. Spears (London, 1901). The remarkable tale was condensed into two short paragraphs.

Curiosity lead to research. Copies of the original manuscript were located in the Archives Nationales, Colonies, Paris, France, and a full translation made.

I.P.

Another illness that played havoc among the human cargoes crowded in the holds of slave ships was the dreaded disease ophthalmia. This disease, once started, spread so fast and with such frightening consequences that in a matter of days whole cargoes of Negroes went blind.

One of the most dramatic cases of an ophthalmic epidemic encompassing an entire ship, slaves, crewmen, and officers, occurred aboard the French slaver, *Le Rodeur*, in the year 1819. The epic tale was recorded by a youthful passenger, a twelve-year-old boy, in a diary intended for his mother. So tragic and heartrending was his poignant tale that it later received widespread attention.

John Greenleaf Whittier, the American poet, used the child's story as a basis for his anti-slavery poem, *The Slave Ships.* The Bibliotheque Ophthalmologique, Paris, devoted prime space in its November 1819 publication to expound on a medical description and analysis of what had transpired on *Le Rodeur* as described by the youngster.

On June 17th, 1820, Deputy M. Benjamin Constant, in a stirring speech before the French Chamber of Deputies, repeated the story in detail and called for the rapid and total abolition of every aspect of Negro slavery under the French flag.

Like other European nations, the French had been very active in the slave trade during the 17th, 18th, and early 19th centuries. The principal French fort and slave factory was Fort Louis, located at the mouth of the River Senegal. There was another important French factory on Goree, an island near Cape Verde.

From these collecting centers, as well as other non-French trading centers on the African coast, thousands of slaves were carried on French slavers to the French possessions, particularly to the sugar plantations in Hispaniola, Guadeloupe, Martinique, and other areas in the French colonial empire.

Young Jacques B. Romaigne begins his eyewitness account with a description of the ship:

"The slaver, *Le Rodeur,* of 200 tons burden, sailed from the port of Havre for the river Calabar on the coast of Africa. She arrived there and anchored at Bonny, March 14, 1819. During a stay of three weeks, she obtained a cargo of 160 Negroes and sailed for Guadeloupe on April 6th, 1819...."

Jacques B. Romaigne, who wrote the account of the epidemic, was the son of a planter from Guadeloupe who had been spending time with relatives in France. His holiday over, he was returning to Guadeloupe as a passenger on *Le Rodeur*, under the special care of the captain. To quote from his diary:

"The Negroes were confined closely to the lower hold and this brought on a disease called ophthalmia which produced blindness.

"The sailors, who sling down provisions from the upper hold, report that the disease is spreading frightfully and today, at dinner, the captain and the surgeon held a conference on the subject. The surgeon declared that from all he could learn, the cases were already so numerous as to be beyond his management.

"The captain insisted that every slave cured was worth his value and that it was better to lose a part than all. The result of the conversation was that the infected slaves were to be transferred to the upper hold and attended by the surgeon.

"All the slaves and some of the crew are blind. The captain, the surgeon and the mate are blind. There are hardly enough men left out of our 22 to work the ship. The captain preserves what order he can and the surgeon still attempts to do his duty, but our situation is frightful.

"All the crew are now blind but one man. The rest work under his orders like unconscious machines, the captain standing by with a thick rope, which he sometimes applies, when led to any recreant by the man who can see.

"My own eyes begin to be affected. In a little while, I shall see nothing but death. I asked the captain if he would not allow the blacks to come up on deck. He said it was no use, that the crew, who were always on deck, were as blind as they; that if brought up, they would only drown themselves, whereas if they remained where they were, they would, in all probability, be at least a portion of them salable, if we had ever the good fortune to reach Guadeloupe.

"We were blind, stone blind, drifting like a wreck upon the ocean and rolling like a cloud before the wind. The captain was

"The Captain, (blind) standing by with a thick rope…" (Walter Appleton Clark, artist)

The crew lay around listless and helpless, one man with sight at the helm
(Walter Appleton Clark, artist)

Blind slaves near rum casks (Walter Appleton Clark, artist)

stone blind, yet had hopes of recovering his sight, while most of the others were in despair.

A guard was continually placed, with drawn swords, at the store room to prevent the men getting at the spirit-casks and dying in a frenzy of intoxication. Some were cursing and swearing from morning till night, some singing abominable songs, some kissing the crucifix and making vows to the blessed saints.

"A few lay all day long in their hammocks, apparently content to starve rather than come abroad for food. For my part, I snatched at anything I could get to eat. Cookery was unthought of. I thought myself fortunate when I was able to procure a cup of water to soften a biscuit as dry and as hard as a stone.

"Mother, your son was blind for ten days, although now so well as to be able to write. I can tell you hardly anything of our history during that period. Each of us lived in a little dark world of his own, peopled by shadows. We did not see the ship, nor the heavens, nor the sea, nor the faces of our comrades.

"Then there came a storm. No hand was upon the helm, not a reef upon the sails. On we flew like a phantom ship of old, that cared not for wind or weather, our masts straining and cracking; our sails bursting from their bonds, with a report like that of musketry; the furious sea one moment devouring us up, stem and stern, and the next casting us forth again, as if with loathing and disgust.

"The wind, at last, died away and we found ourselves, rocking without motion, on the sullen deep. . . ."

It was at this time that a sail was sighted, and the one man who had the use of his eyes steered *Le Rodeur* toward her. The oncoming vessel turned out to be a drifting derelict with all sail set, though men were wandering her deck. The young Romaigne tells what followed in a most dramatic fashion:

"We heard a sound upon the waters. Our hearts burst with hope. We held our breath. The sound continued. It was like the splashing of a heavy body in smooth water. A cry arose from every lip on deck and was echoed by the men in their hammocks below and by the slaves in the hold.

"Our cry was answered! We shouted again, our voices broken by sobs and our burning eyes deluged with tears. Our captain was the first to recover his self possession. We heard him speak the approaching ship with the usual challenge:

"'Ship Ahoy! Ahoy! What ship?'

"'The *Saint Leon* of Spain. Help us for God's sake!'

"'We want help ourselves,' replied our captain.

"And from the Spaniard: 'We are dying of hunger and thirst. Send us on board some provisions and a few hands to work the ship and name your own terms. . . .'

"Answered our Captain: 'We can give you food, but we are in want of hands ourselves. Come on board of us and we will exchange provisions with you for men. . . .'

"And from the Spaniard: 'Dollars! dollars! We will pay you in money, a thousand fold, but we cannot send men. We have Negroes on board. They have infected us with ophthalmia, and we are all stone-blind . . . !'

"At the announcement of this horrible coincidence, there was a silence among us, like that of death. It was broken by a fit of laughter on our ship, in which I joined. Before our awful merriment was over, we could hear by the sound of curses which the Spaniards shouted against us, that the *Saint Leon* drifted away. The vessel, in all probability, foundered at sea. She was never heard from again. . . .

"The man who preserved his sight the longest, recovered the soonest. To his exertions alone we owe that we are now within a few leagues of Guadeloupe, this 21st day of June, 1819.

"I am almost well. The surgeon and eleven more are irrecoverably blind. The captain has lost one eye. Four others have met with the same calamity. Five are able to see, though dimly, with both. Among the slaves, 39 are completely blind and the rest blind of one eye or their sight otherwise injured. . . ."

Sources

1. John R. Spears, *The American Slave Trade* (London: 1901).

2. Jaccques B. Romaigne Diary, 1819, Archives Nationales, Colonies Paris, France.

3. Bibliotheque Ophthalmologique, *Publication* (November, 1819).

4. French Chamber of Deputies, *Bulletin*, Paris, France (June 17, 1820).

VI
Influence of Moravian Missionaries

Records in the Danish State Archives give us a good account of how slave cargoes were handled:

"A few days out of St. Thomas, the miserable victims must have sensed that the voyage was nearing an end. Food rations were increased. Grown-ups, male and female, got tobacco and pipes. This improvement of food and treatment was, usually, an attempt to fatten the cargoes and put the enslaved ones in a good frame of mind for the impending auctions.

"After the arrival in St. Thomas, the Negroes were taken ashore and stored in large warehouses. They were grouped according to nationality.

I.P.

Christian Georg Andreas Oldendorp, the Moravian scholar, tells us that when he arrived in St. Thomas (May 1761), Negro slaves on that island were from the following tribes and places in Africa:

"Mandinga, Kanga, Loango, Congo, Amina, Papaa, Ibo, Bibi, Karabari, Watje, Kassenti, Selungo, Fida and Fulah...."

Oldendorp described the St. Thomas Negroes of that period, with the exception of Moravian converts, as being "without religious practices." He mentioned, however, a kind of initiation ceremony which the established slaves had for the newcomers.

"These newly-arrived ones were paraded, made to form circles, and chanted over in the Congo tongue. They were then given several symbolic lashes across the back and shoulders to atone for their evil doings in the African countries from whence they came.

This ceremony, Oldendorp thought, had no relationship to religion but was meant to provide the newcomers with godparents who would help them to adjust to their new surroundings as slaves.

Oldendorp declared that most of the slaves brought to St. Thomas had been captured in inter-tribal warfare. They came from all levels of African societies.

"These St. Thomas slaves presented a mixed company of rich and poor, high and mighty, and lesser persons; the latter, serfs in the society from which they came," Oldendorp noted.

"The condition of slavery had done for these uprooted African societies *what death does for all men;* it had flattened them to a common level, kings, queens, children of princes, nobles, tradesmen. Slavery had set them in a kind of rigid equality.

"Some slaves of noble birth," wrote Oldendorp, "found it impossible to adjust themselves to their reduced circumstances. A Negro Queen, full of memories of her former greatness, refused to submit herself to her island Mistress: 'I was much greater in Guinea than you are here, she said, 'I had many more slaves than you have. Now you expect me to be your slave? I would rather starve to death...!'

Group of slaves just landed, to be auctioned (Stedman's *Narrative of an Expedition*, London, 1796)

"She carried out the determination, completely indifferent to harshness or leniency, and died a lingering death."

Oldendorp gave another example. A distinguished Negro, member of a noble family on the Guinea coast, had been seized by traders and sold with all of his slaves as a vassal This man's fate differed from the others on the Middle Passage in that he kept his clothing, was free of chains on the ship, ate with the whites at the Captain's table, and was sold in the Danish islands not in open auction but to a good master, privately.

Even in his slavery in St. Thomas, the vassals of his family respected him. He, on the other hand, did all he could to lessen the hardship of their condition."

The remarkable differences in quality and character among the St. Thomas slaves was described by Oldendorp:

"Some slaves absolutely refused to work and had to be dealt with in a very firm manner. This high degree of strong will and refusal to bend was most prominent among the Karabari, Ibo, Bibi and Amina Negroes.

On the other hand, willingness to serve were especially found among the Watje, Kassenti, Congo, Selungo, Fida, and Papaa tribes. The price of slaves from these latter groups was higher as a result of this fact."

On April 9, 1764, King Frederik V of Denmark declared St. Thomas a free port for vessels of all nations. As a result, St. Thomas became a hub, a transshipment center, not only for manufactured goods and agricultural products but for Negro cargoes as well. Trafficking in slaves became big business.

Vessels, flying the flags of many nations, interlopers of all sizes and descriptions, crowded the harbor of St. Thomas with their live cargoes.

In his *History, Civil and Commercial, of the British Colonies in the West Indies*, (London, 1793-1794) Bryan Edwards estimated that during the 18th century well over two million slaves were imported into the British West Indies alone.

Were we to add the slave cargoes carried by Dutch, Portugese, Spanish, French, Brandenburgers, Danish traders, as well as nondescript unknown nationals, the totals would be staggering.

This traffic in human flesh, to be as great as it was, needed organization, and that organization was supplied by many of the so-called civilized nations of Europe and to a lesser but effective degree by the independents, the so-called "interlopers"— ship captains and adventurers eager to get a "piece of the action."

These unauthorized interlopers, who dashed in and out of the slave areas on the West African Coast assigned to government monopolies and chartered companies, did a surprisingly large share of the business.

It is estimated that a large percentage of the Negro slaves brought to St. Thomas and sold on this island were brought here by interlopers. Recognizing their inability to do very much to stop this illicit trade, island officials followed the axiom: "If you can't lick it, join it!"

Setting themselves up as "middlemen," Danish officials did not permit the island planters to buy directly from the interloper captains. Everything had to be done through "official" channels. No slave could be landed without payment of an import duty set at 4 percent. Officials also frequently bought numbers of slaves for customers in other islands. Large fortunes were made in St. Thomas this way.

Behavioral habits of certain Negroes were known well in advance and adversely affected the demand for them and the price.

Slaves of New Calabar, for instance, were known to be "slothful, cruel in temper, always quarreling, biting and fighting; sometimes choking and murdering each other without mercy." There was a common belief among ship captains that "whoever carried New Calabar slaves to the West Indies had need to pray for a quick passage."

Negroes from Accra, tribesmen and women from Dahomey, Ashanti, Sherbros, Fellatahs, and Bambarras were much in demand. They were strong and durable and, once adjusted, fitted well into the overall slave economy.

Negroes from the Mandingo tribe were known for their speed in adjusting and acquiring skills. They made excellent artisans and craftsmen and were eagerly sought after at the auctions.

So were the Negroes from the nations of Kassaos, Fi, and the Sherbroo Buttom people. They were finely built, intelligent men and women.

This was particularly true of the Foulah women from Timbo. Not only were their courage and resistance a byword on the slavers, but of all the African women, they were most desired by the Europeans.

Capt. Theodore Canot, who considered himself a connoisseur of women, wrote in high praise of the Foulah females.

He had gone to Timbo on a slave collecting mission and had been most attracted to the shapely women. When he tried to approach them, they fled no doubt because his reputation for the ladies preceded him.

Towards nightfall Canot left his companions, wrapped himself in a Mandingo dress, and stole away through byways to a brook which ran by the town walls. It was here that the females of Timbo came at sunset to draw water. Canot hid himself where he could not be seen and for more than an hour watched the graceful Foulah girls and women.

"Unaware of my presence, they came forth in a simple dress which covers the body from waist to knee, and leaves the rest of the figure entirely naked.

"I do not think the forms of these Foulah girls are exceeded in symmetry by the women of any other country. They had a slender delicacy of limb, wrist, neck, hand, foot and bosom. None were deformed nor were any marked by traces of disease...."

Historians concede that Christian Georg Andreas Oldendorp's *Geschichte der Mission der Evangelischen Bruder auf der Carabaischen Inseln, St. Thomas, St. Croix and St. John* (1777), is the most accurate and comprehensive account of the early history of the Moravian brethren in the Danish West Indies. It is the fountain-head from which later-day historians drew and continue to draw source material.

One such historian was the Lutheran parson and Christiansted resident, Herman C. Johannes Lawaetz (1890-1903). Years of research into early Moravian history, and particularly the works of Oldendorp, culminated in the publication, of

Negro slaves from Loango (Stedman's *Narrative of an Expedition*, London, 1796)

Lawaetz's, *Brodremenighedens Mission, Dansk-Vestindien,* 1769-1848, (Kjobenhavn, 1902); a summary of the early Moravian missionary efforts in the Danish West Indies. We select and condense from this document:

"In preaching to the slaves about the virtues of submission and obedience to their masters, the Moravian missionaries went against the interests of the island planters at one point only. A female slave who had been baptized must not, even against the worst threats, give in to her master!

On this point, the Brethren were inflexible. They looked upon chastity as the most important of all virtues.

The emphasis on chastity, in missionary teachings to the baptized slaves, was an outgrowth of a concept of chastity, practiced in the Moravian establishment at Herrnhut, Saxony.

In the light of the missionary having to reject his own personal feelings, having to, in fact, freeze his innermost desires and emotions, one can imagine the almost impossible task facing the early missionaries when they came to the Danish West India islands.

Little wonder the religious zealots incurred the early wrath of the white planters. Here was a privileged class, masters of a colonial society in which they thrived; excessively promiscuous in sexual behavior; excessively indulgent in personal patterns of everyday living that to the tightly disciplined missionary appeared to be glaringly sinful.

How could a privileged planter react, except in anger, to alien preachers advocating moral abstinence, rigid limitation of personal excesses and chastity, even in marriage. Moravian doctrines must have sounded like pure idiocy to those planters.

What about the slaves in that early period? Torn from their African roots, haunted by fear of the overseer's whip, treated as less than human beings; deprived of dignity, traded like cattle, how could they react to emotional suppression; how could they react, for instance, to the sheer concept of chastity?

If there was anything that a master, an overseer, or a bomba could not take away from the slaves was their sensuality.

History has shown us that the down-trodden, the economically deprived, the locked-in sub-strata of a society, resort to sensuality as an escape.

The African slave expressed his powerful sensuality in his dances, his way of life, his promiscuity. And here were preachers advocating that the slave surrender his most powerful outlet for the *now* in exchange for the rewards of an afterlife. It was little wonder that the missionary's main converts were old people and children.

Oldendorp had this to say about children born to slaves on the plantations:

"The Negroes are very solicitous in the care of their infants. Superstition makes them very much afraid that through some *supernatural power* the newly-born child may lose his health or even his life.

"The 8th day after the birth is considered very dangerous. On that day the child's father, his relatives and friends, set up a watchful vigil from early hours of the morning until well past midnight. The hour of midnight is the critical one.

"The overwhelming fear is that one of the many evil and invisible denizens of the spirit world who thrive best on mother's milk will slip by the guard of father, friends and relatives, to affix his toothless gums to the full breast of the mother *and suck it dry!*

"Not only will this draining of the mother deprive the newborn child of vital nourishment, but the toothless gums of the evil spirit are known to leave a residue of poison on the emptied breast.

"Should the hungry baby so much as touch with its lips this contaminated area of mother's flesh, then the child will, without fail, wither and die within a matter of days...."

Earlier and later historians, from Oldendorp (1777) to the Lutheran scholar, Jens Larsen (1950), tell us that the unique Negro Dutch Creole dialect spoken in the Danish West Indies originated in St. Thomas.

Oldendorp records that when he arrived in St. Thomas, (mid-18th century), so many languages were being spoken that the island was a veritable Tower of Babel. Oldendorp mentions 26 different dialects found among slaves on St. Thomas, most of whom had come from the hinterland of West Africa and through the African port city of Loanda.

A Dutch trader visiting the island a short time after Olden-dorp tells us that during a disastrous fire that threatened to destroy a large part of the old city, he heard frantic cries of 'FIRE' expressed in more than one dozen languages."

Larsen, the 20th century historian, sums up the communication problem of that period this way:

"Slaves that first came to St. Thomas in large numbers spoke many languages because they came from many different tribes and regions of Africa."

Add to this the problem of settlers and traders coming to the island from Holland, France, Germany, Denmark, England, Spain, Portugal, etc., each and everyone speaking in his own tongue. One can imagine the confusion and the need for a common language understandable by slaves as well as their owners.

Out of this need, came an answer: the Negro Dutch Creole dialect of the Danish West India islands. And why Dutch Creole? Let the historian, Larsen, answer that question:

"Because the majority of the plantation owners in the Danish West India islands at that time were Dutch nationals. They taught their slaves Dutch! They were assisted in this by slaves brought to St. Thomas by Dutch owners from other Dutch islands, slaves who already knew some Dutch words and expressions...."

Larsen continued: "New slaves arriving from Africa to the Danish islands learned the Dutch 'patois' both from their owners and from fellow slaves."

The fact that Danes, Germans, French, Spanish and Por-tugese mixed a few words of their own with the Dutch, accounts for the presence of such foreign words in the Negro Dutch Creole dialect, but overall the Dutch language dominated.

"This newly formed pidgin Dutch dialect underwent constant modifications," noted Larsen, "as the slave owners improved on it, here and there, and as the slaves continued to give it their African touch in sentence construction and soft musical tone, softening the harsh guttural sounds of the Europeans."

Via Dutch settlers, Negro Dutch Creole was carried to St. Croix and St. John, where it spread widely, not only among the Negroes but also among the white people whose children learned it from their Negro nursemaids.

A Watchful Vigil (Author's private collection)

Soldiers, prompted by planters, breaking up a missionary prayer meeting
(The Moravian Archives, Saxony, Germany)

Creool Psalm Buk (The Moravian Archives, Saxony, Germany)

20

Een kleintje Kint, O Blitkap rik
Ka parie voor ons na Gront,
Yt een Meisje skoon en heilig,
Alleen for wees ons Heilant;
As Godt sie Soon die Mensheit no
ha neem an,
Ons almael sa ha mut verlooren
gaen,
Hem bin die Saeligheit van ons alle;
Ons le dank Ju sutte Jesu,
Dat Ju een Mens ka kom, O nu
Bewaer ons van die Helle.

Melodie. J Jesu Navn.

I.

Na Jesu Naem
Al ons Werk sa geskiet,
As die beqwaem voor ons, en son-
der Skaem
Sa tot ons best kom yt;
Want almael gut,
Sa wees, en loop heel sut.
Die

(o) 21

Die na die ka begin,
Tee die die Meet le vind,
Dat tot Godt sie Eer die bin,
En ons self sa Seegen vind,
Na wat gut ons ook begin.
2.
Na Jesu Naem
Ons wil nu pries ons Godt,
Hem self sa maek ons ook datue be-
qwaem,
For due al na sie Gebot;
Hem soo groot Werk
Ka maek mit sie Woort sterk,
En mit sie groote Kragt
Ka toon soo mussie Magt,
Die maek ons mut altit
Geg hem Dankie mit groot Vlit,
Die le vrees die Heer gief agt.
3.
Na Jesu Naem
Ons wil for leef en doot,
As ons sa leef, die wees dan sonder
Blaem,
As ons sa sterf, ons no kom na Noot;
Na Jesu Naem
Tot sie Eer, maer niet ons Skaem,
Ons

Creool Hymn (The Moravian Archives, Saxony, Germany)

One of the characteristics of Negro Dutch Creole" stated Larsen, "is simplification, the discarding of words not absolutely necessary to the meaning of the sentence. Here is an example: 'The crocodile is not afraid of the snake; the snake is not afraid of the crocodile.' Translated into simplified Dutch Creole, this becomes: *'Croc no bang slang; slang no bang croc...!'*

"Here is another example 'One finger cannot catch lice.' Translated into Dutch Creole: *'Een vinger no kan vang loes...!'* Again: 'Cockroach does not belong in chicken house.' Dutch Creole: *'Kakerlak no hat recht na hoenerkot...!'*

"Words of African origin in Negro Dutch Creole are taken chiefly from names of products of the vegetable and animal kingdom. For example: *'geambo,'* fruit; *'jekke,'* guinea fowl; *'karang,'* name of a fish; *'kingamboe,'* okra; *'tschikki,'* jigger, a ground flea which buries itself under the toenail....!

"Some examples of English words in Negro Dutch Creole are: *'dig,'* *'jump,'* *'krop,'* or *'crop;'* *'trubel,'* or *'trouble,'* *'vens'*, or *'fence'*...!

"Some examples of Spanish words in Negro Dutch Creole are *'adios,'* goodbye; *'cabrita,'* goat; *'kawai*, horse; *'pat-tal'*, duck; *'savan,'* field....!

"Less numerous in Negro Dutch Creole are words of Portugese origin. Here are a few: *'bussal'*, a Negro born in Africa. *'traval,'* trouble, pain."

According to Larsen, Oldendorp tried to describe the simplicity of the Negro Dutch Creole. Everything was made easier. Words were shorter. There was only one gender. Plural is formed by adding *'en.'* *'Mi ha'* meant (I have); *'Mi a ha,'* (I had). 'Mi ka ha', (I have had). *'Mi sal ha,'* (I will have).

The sheer simplicity of Negro Dutch Creole made a scholar like Oldendorp anxious. Was this really a good enough language in which to spread God's word? Was it at all possible to translate complex parts of the Bible to this strange mixture of languages?

Oldendorp and other Moravian linguists realized soon that the road to the Negro's heart and understanding was through this simple Creole language. They had no other choice than to work with it and further improve it.

One of the earliest and most effective uses of the improved Creole language was the use of it in the speech made by Count Zinzendorf on the eve of his departure from St. Thomas for Europe, February 15, 1739.

Zinzendorf addressed a huge mass meeting of Negro converts at Mosquito Bay (now Lindbergh Bay). Delivered entirely in Negro Dutch Creole, the speech had been prepared for Zinzendorf by Johann Lorentz Carstens, the St. Thomas planter and great friend of the Moravians.

Another early and effective use of the improved Negro Dutch Creole was in the two petitions given to Count Zinzendorf to deliver in person to the King and Queen of Denmark.

These petitions prepared entirely in Negro Dutch Creole and written by Negro men and women slaves prayed of the Danish rulers the right to be instructed in a religion of their own choice; and for protection from bodily harm while doing so.

Jens Larsen also tells us that Danish Lutheran translations into Creole began with Johannes Christian Kingo, first Lutheran missionary to St. Thomas. (1757-1782).

Soon after his arrival in St. Thomas, Kingo prepared a Creole dictionary to help him communicate with the Negroes. He continued to work on translating biblical passages into Creole with his efforts culminating in a primer, the *Kreoal A-B-C Book* (1770).

Jens Larsen continues:

There was probably no other place in the world at the time where so high a proportion of the slaves could read as in the Danish West India islands.

It is impossible to measure the influence of the Negro Dutch Creole literature produced by the missionaries, both Moravian and Lutheran. One fact is clear. It gave the Negroes a new sense of dignity. It helped to mold them from a number of diverse groups into a homogeneous people," concludes Larsen.

Through the medium of Negro Dutch Creole numerous Negroes in the Danish islands learned to read, write, and sing in this adopted language three quarters of a century before Emancipation became a reality.

Sources

1. Christian Georg Andreas Oldendorp, *Geschichte der Mission der evangelischen Bruder auf del Carabaischen Inseln, St. Thomas, St. Croix, St. Jan* (Barby: 1777).

2. Herman C. Johannes Lawaetz, *Brodremenighrdens Mission, Dansk-Vestindien, 1769-1848* (Copenhagen: 1902).

3. A. von Dewitz, *In Danisch Westindien, Anfange der Brudermission in St. Thomas, St. Croix, and St. Jan, 1732-1760* (Herrnhut: 1899).

4. *Creool Psalm-Buk voor die Deen Missioon na Westindien* (Copenhagen: 1770).

5. E.V. Lose, *Kort Udsigt over den danske Lutherske Missions Historie paa St. Croix, St. Thomas, og St. Jan* (Copenhagen: 1890).

6. Johannes Christion Kingo, *Kreool A-B-C Buk* (St. Croix: 1770).

7. Jens Larsen, *The Virgin Islands Story* (Philadelphia: 1950).

VII

Johan Lorenz Carstens, St. Thomas Planter, Friend of the Missionaries

From the early part of the 18th century, the Moravian missionaries of Herrnhut, Saxony, a province of Germany, exerted a profound influence on the Negro slaves of the Danish West Indies.

It all started when religious refugees from Moravia, a sect known as the Moravian brethren, found asylum on the estate of Count Nikolaus Ludwig von Zinzendorf, a pious nobleman, who devoted his life to Protestant religious causes.

To this spacious estate of Berthelsdorf, Saxony, came remnants of the original Moravian brotherhood from Moravia, Bavaria, and other parts of Germany. When the refugees were strong enough, June 17, 1722, they began to build a town named Herrnhut, which means, "The charge of the Lord."

As the colony grew, the brethren reemphasized christian unity and personal service. They showed zeal in religious preparation and sent missionaries to Denmark, Switzerland, central Germany, and the Danish West Indies (1732).

The success of the Moravian missionaries in St. Thomas in winning over slaves embittered a considerable number of local planters. They feared that spread of the Moravian concept of brotherhood might lead to social upheaval in St. Thomas, if not outright revolts as a result of Moravian teaching.

The planters were endeavoring to destroy the Moravian mission and its missionaries when an event occurred which altered the situation. Count Zinzendorf set sail from Europe for St. Thomas. On January 29, 1739, his ship came into the harbor and anchored.

The news of Zinzendorf's arrival spread like wildfire and

created great excitement. From lip to lip, from shanty to shanty, the message rang, "The Count is here."

Zinzendorf's name was like a magician's wand. The sound of it wrought wonderous changes. He had come, the great leader of missions, all the way from Saxony, Germany, to this tiny island of St. Thomas to see fair play established between the oppressors and the oppressed.

In the three weeks that he was on St. Thomas, Count Zinzendorf did much to quiet the situation. He sought and received assurances from island authorities that they would no longer stand idly by while the missionaries and their converts were being molested.

I.P.

Count Nikolaus L. von Zinzendorf, 1700–1760, head of the Moravian Brethern, Herrnhut, Saxony. (The Moravian Archives Saxony, Germany)

(Oval) Carl Adolph von Plessen, 1678–1758, by A. Manyocki (Fredericksborg, Museum, Denmark)

When Count Zinzendorf left for Europe, he took with him petitions from Negro slaves to be presented to the King of Denmark praying for the right of slaves to be instructed in the religion of their choice.

On August 7, 1739, Count Zinzendorf secured from the Danish Court written assurances of religious liberty for the slaves and protection for the Moravian missionaries.

Shortly after Count Zinzendorf left St. Thomas (February 17, 1739) and returned to Europe, the Moravian missionaries on the island lost another friend and protector, Johan Lorentz Carstens. He, too, left for Europe (1739) to permanently settle in Denmark.

Johan Lorentz Carstens was born in St. Thomas in the year 1705. He was named after his uncle, Governor Johan Lorentz, who assumed the governship in 1690 and died in office 12 years later (1702). Carstens marriage to Jacoba Von Holten, daughter of Governor Joachim Von Holten, (1706-1709) combined the wealth of two governors and some of the wealthiest plantations in St. Thomas.

Danish historians tell us that as early as 1733, Johan Lorentz Carstens had journeyed to Copenhagen to get permission from the West India and Guinea Company to transfer the bulk of his fortune from St. Thomas to Denmark.

A main reason for the desired change of residence was that the West Indian climate did not agree with Carstens's wife, Jacoba. She had lost two children shortly after birth, and her health had remained very fragile ever since.

However, when Carstens arrived in Denmark (August 1733), the treaty of purchase of St. Croix had been signed (June 15, 1733) and ratified by Louis XV of France just 13 days later (June 28, 1733).

Two of the key negotiators for the Danish West India and Guinea Company, Privy Councilor Carl Adolf von Plessen and Frederick Holmsted, Mayor of Copenhagen, leaned heavily on Carstens's intimate knowledge of the newly acquired West Indian island of St. Croix. Instead of encouraging him to come back to Denmark, they urged him to return to the islands and act as an adviser to many influential people in the Danish capital who were acquiring land in St. Croix and investing heavily there. They rewarded Carstens for his help and counsel with a sizeable grant of land in St. Croix.

The Moravian scholar John Holmes tells us that the "insider" in the purchase of St. Croix, Lord Chamberlain, Count Carl Adolf von Plessen, acquired six large estates on that island.

A close friend and admirer of Count Zinzendorf, von Plessen applied to the Count for 12 Moravian brethren, or two overseers for each of his six plantations on St. Croix.

Von Plessen knew that the Moravian brethren were a powerful influence urging their converts to accept their lot in this world and to pray for redemption in the next. With Moravian help, von Plessen could foresee a stable work force on his plantations.

Von Plessen's request was no sooner made known to the congregation at Herrnhut than a number of brethren and sisters offered themselves to form a colony in St. Croix using their strategic positions as overseers to preach the Gospel to the slaves.

These were the 14 missionaries who arrived in St. Thomas on the 11th of June, 1734, on their way to St. Croix.

It was through the influence of Lord Chamberlain, Count Carl Adolf von Plessen, during the years 1733-1734 that Johan Lorentz Carstens became such an early and staunch supporter of the Moravian brethren.

After his return to St. Thomas from Copenhagen, Carstens and his wife, Jacoba, stood as godfather and godmother to one of the Moravian baptized slaves, a young Negro named Domingo. This was an open act of courage at that time in the face of blind and unyielding planter hostility to the Moravian missionaries.

Danish historians note that Johan Lorentz Carstens's business prospered greatly in the years 1735-1739. His slaves now worked on all three islands: St. Thomas, St. Croix, and St. John. He had several ships, among them the brig *Mrs. Jacoba*, taking his products to America, Holland, and Denmark:

"Everything Carstens did in business during that period succeeded. Only his family life failed him. Still another daughter died shortly after birth. Jacoba's health became increasingly

Moravian mission station Friedensthal, St. Croix. (The Moravian
Archives Saxony, Germany)

View of Moravian settlement near Fredericksted, Henry Morton's
Sketchbook 1843–1844 (Courtesy The St. Croix Landmarks Society)

Johan Lorentz Carstens, 1705–1747 (Fredericksborg Castle, Denmark)

Knabstrup estate and Mansion (The Royal Library, Kobenhavn, Denmark)

weaker and in 1739 Carstens determined to carry out his earlier plans to settle with his family in Denmark.

"He carefully chose managers for his plantations and left St. Thomas with his wife, his only living daughter, Anna Maria, and very specially picked slaves from St. Thomas.

"The sea voyage had a tonic effect on Jacoba. By the time they arrived in Amsterdam, she was feeling much stronger. From Amsterdam, they travelled to Saxony to visit Count Zinzendorf. In October 1739, they reached Copenhagen and settled there.

"The 34-year-old planter from St. Thomas became a citizen of Copenhagen, but his business on the islands still occupied most of his time. Shortly after his arrival in Denmark, he purchased a new ship that he put into the island traffic.

"In little or no time, Carstens became a recognized European authority on the Danish West Indian islands. Among others, Christian VI, himself, sought his advice concerning the management of the new Royal plantations on St. Croix.

"Carstens prepared for the Danish King a detailed description of life among the Negro slaves in the islands.

Carstens and his wife, Jacoba, became natural members of an aristocratic inner circle who ran the sugar and slave business at that time. When Jacoba gave birth to a boy, he was named after the president of the West India and Guinea Company, Carl Adolf von Plessen. This very influential man personally attended the baptismal ceremony as godfather. So did another powerful director of the Company, Justice Advisor Frederik Holmsted.

"Carstens bought a farm, 'Farumgaard,' with a beautiful residence on it. He sold this farm in 1743 and purchased a larger and very impressive estate, 'Knabstrup.'"

By this time, Johan Lorentz Carstens had been made a nobleman and given the aristocratic name, Castenschiold. Needing more laborers, he carefully picked slaves from St. Thomas.

"On his estate, 'Knabstrup,' Carstens constructed model quarters for his Negroes. Today, these quarters still stand and are called, 'the St. Thomas houses.'

"The Carstens (Castenschiold) family kept in close touch

with friends in the islands including their favorite slaves. Among the family heirlooms are several letters from the slave Domingo, whose baptism they had attended and for whom they had stood as godparents. Domingo wrote:

"'I hope that these lines reach the Master, the Mistress, the little Miss and the young gentleman, and find them in good health. I greet you from Cattie and Mintie and all the Negroes who have been baptized and who love Jesus....'

"Domingo sent the 'very much honoured Miss Anna Maria,' a small box containing sugar-cakes."

Johan Lorentz Carstens (Castenschiold) died June 19, 1747, at the age of 42. An epidemic of smallpox had spread through the countryside and had come to the Castenschiold estate. First to succomb was Castenschiold's little son. Then the father contracted the disease and after a brief illness succombed. He left holdings in Denmark and the West India islands valued at millions of dollars.

According to Danish historians, weird stories circulated in the Danish countryside about Castenschiold on the night of his death. These stories were attributed to an old man on the farm, Hans Nielsen.

"Hans had worked at Knabstrup all his life. During the winters, he attended the cows and in the summers he performed routine chores. On the night of Castenschiold's death, Hans Nielsen was awakened by the sounds of horses galloping into the yard and stopping at the great house.

"Nielsen got up from his bed and moved cautiously to the stable. From a corner of it, he got a good view of the happenings taking place at the entrance of the residence.

"There before him, as clear as could be, he saw a black carriage drawn by four black horses. The coachman in the driver's box was black and the footman at the rear was black.

"There was extreme silence for a short time and then there was movement. A gentleman, elegantly dressed, stepped from the doorway, crossed the step and entered the carriage.

"The coachman, black from head to toe, lifted the reins, turned horses and carriage around, urged the horses into a gallop and disappeared into the night.

"Next day, Hans Nielsen learned that the master of the estate,

Johan Lorentz Castenschiold, had died at the exact hour that he had witnessed the incident described.

"For some time, Hans Nielsen told the story of what he had seen to anyone who would listen to him. There was no question in his simple mind that West Indian slaves had come for their master to take him away in elegant style.

"'Though these black people looked like human beings,' Hans Nielsen said, *'they were not real people...!'*"

In 1742, three years after he settled in Denmark, and upon the request of Christian VI, Johan Lorentz Carstens prepared for the Danish King a detailed, eyewitness account of life among the Negro slaves of the Danish West India islands of St. Thomas and St. John.

The manuscript, 198 pages in length, was evidently prepared while Carstens was still living at "Farumgaard." Written in a handsome, even hand, without a single correction, the manuscript lay hidden in the Danish State Archives of Sea Maps since the 18th century.

It was discovered by a scholar as recently as 1928 and turned over to the Danish Navy Library. We select and condense portions from this historical document:

"The black inhabitants of the islands, St. Thomas-St. John, are divided into four classes: The free-Negroes, the house-slaves, the plantation slaves and the maroon-Negroes.

"Most of the free-Negroes are mulattoes. Including women, they number about 500. Some of these free-Negroes acquired their freedom after their master's or mistress's death by last will or testament.

"Other free-Negroes are those who bought their freedom from their masters. Usually it costs a slave 500 to 900 Riksdollars to buy his freedom, but there are cases where slaves have had to pay as much as 1300 Riksdollars.

"This has occurred where the master discovered that because the slave in question was thrifty, industrious, hardworking, young and strong, he had accumulated savings. In situations of this kind, the masters argue that whatever the slave owned at the time of the transaction, whether it be a physical body, money, or possessions were part of the master's assets...

"The rest of the black inhabitants, who are not free, are slaves, thralls, and serfs. Their bodies are used for service, or for whatever purpose the master wants.

"The house-slaves are the most outstanding. They perform all the duties in the home. The master has his male slaves, the mistress her female slaves, and the children have theirs.

"In the large mansions, it is not unusual to find 16 to 24 such waiters or servants. An ordinary house has from four to six. These slaves, male or female, have to be in readiness at all times to serve whether their master or mistress sits, lies, walks, or travels.

"Because of mosquitoes which are a steady nuisance for people all over the islands, slaves at evening time, or siesta, have to stir the air above their masters or mistresses until they fall asleep. Slaves use a thickly leafed branch, like a fan, for this purpose.

"When a mistress is riding horse-back in the countryside, up and down hills, male slaves have to follow on foot, running as rapidly as the mistress is riding. Those who are able, hold to the horsetails.

"Persons who do not own slaves themselves, but need them for housework, rent them from owners. Costs are seven to eight Riksdollars a month, besides food for the slave. Through such servants, slaves earn for their masters considerably more than the cost to keep them per day.

"One may also hire a free-Negro for five Riksdollars per month, but they are not as submissive as those who are owned and rented out because of the latter's fear of a master's punishment.

"Special house-slaves also have to perform very personal services. When masters or mistresses, on behalf of nature, have to relieve themselves in their secret rooms, then a slave or slave woman, for a sake of their master's or mistress' convenience, stand by with a 'whisk.'

"This is a cutoff maiz stick, three ell long, with a round soft tuft at the end. When nature has been satisfied, then the slave, or the slave woman dries the master or mistress with the 'whisk.'

"House-slaves are generally superior in intellect and manners to plantation slaves. They believe that God is in Heaven,

Slaves performing routine household tasks (Courtesy Mapes Monde Co., Ltd., Rome)

they believe in an immortal soul, they are polite, modest, and service-minded.

"These house-slaves regard upper-class whites highly. Many female house-slaves, when they get the chance, by signs and gestures, offer themselves in intercourse and seduce many of our young European males from the best families.

"On the other hand, the more religious house-slaves look up to virtuous white Christians and try to imitate them. These religious ones, as part of their religious training, become lovers of certain virtues, such as honesty, candidness, and soberness.

"The third group are the plantation-slaves. They show a far coarser and wilder behavior than the house-slaves. Many of them are brought in from Africa, and they are as different as the many landscapes and areas of Africa from which they come.

Slaves cutting sugar cane under supervision (Author's private collection)

Slaves bringing cane to the mill, Henry Morton Sketchbook, 1834–1844
(Courtesy The St. Croix Landmarks Society)

Slaves fueling the boilers (Courtesy Mapes Monde Co. Ltd., Rome)

Slaves ladling sugar syrup (Courtesy Mapes Monde Co. Ltd., Rome)

Another slave workers scene (Author's private collection)

Slave workers toil while bombas supervise (Courtesy: Mapes Monde Co. Ltd., Rome)

"These alien slaves from all kinds of tribes, when they are brought to the islands, are called *bussals*, which means in their language *stranger* or *foreigner*.

"Some of these *bussals* are idolaters. They worship the sun, the moon, the stars, the earth, lightning. Some have a god for every day; the first thing they meet in the morning, whether it be a bird, animal, even a tree . . . they worship this object throughout the day.

"Others of these people are completely without religion. They do not want to know of any god or idols. They act like animals. They are wild and prone to murder. This is especially true of Negroes from El Mina. These belong to an unruly and barbaric tribe, a warrior people against all others.

"El Minas are so wilful and tyrannical that if one orders them to do something they oppose, or gives them something to eat they do not want, they right away kill themselves. They say nothing, remain sullen, and suddenly take a sharp instrument and put it into their bowels and die right away. Therefore, one has to be careful in dealing with them.

"El Mina slaves are the strongest. They can pull or carry weights like mules. Two of those belonging to that tribe have been known to lift 900 pounds with their bare hands.

"There are strong witch-masters among these plantation-slaves. They brought their witchcraft with them from Africa. They can put into people a lump of twisted hair, cut-off nails, or sharp thin pieces of rusted iron and in a short time their victim dies.

"Some of these witch-masters have been known to shrink people in size. Others have been known to turn away bullets fired directly at them.

"There are many plantation slaves who are industrious, practical, and well behaved. They take care of themselves with food and clothes. They receive nothing from their masters but a small piece of ground which they cultivate skillfully.

"Work hours in the field are long, from 5 o'clock in the morning until 6:30 in the evening. These field-workers are supervised by bombas who follow closely behind them with 'silkefalle,' or whips made of twisted ox-hide.

"Under supervision of bombas, groups of these field workers

alternate at night in keeping watch near the houses and over the cattle to prevent maroon, or runaway slaves, who hide in the bush during the day, from stealing such cattle or breaking into the houses.

"The bomba's job is to look closely over everything that is taking place on the plantation and to report to the overseer, who, in turn, reports to the masters. The bomba's reward is that he is free from all kinds of menial labor. As a sign that he is different and special, he carries his 'silkefalle,' or whip, at all times. On the plantations, there is usually a bomba to every 50 slaves."

Nineteenth-century historians, both Danish and British, had a good deal to say about death on the plantation and the funerals that followed. In most cases, these historians concurred that the stark reality of death seemed to awaken in plantation Negroes superstitions and instincts that surely went back to their African origins.

Pallbearers and mourners generally gathered about the *"hut of the dead,"* hours before the slave-funeral began. Dressed in white and barefooted, bearers discussed with each other a transport plan of action before raising the coffin to their shoulders.

In the event that the corpse be that of a matured and well respected person, it was not uncommon for the leader of the pallbearers to take time (in a one-way conversation) to discuss with the dead one the exact road upon which it wished to be carried.

In some cases, it was reported, the corpse absolutely and silently refused to go past the habitation of former enemies. Then, no human power could force it to do so. If the pallbearers insisted on following a course contrary to the wishes of the dead, corpse and coffin had been known to jump off the shoulders of the bearers.

In passing along a wooded trail, Negro slave-funeral processions often came to a halt while bearers lowered the coffin to the ground in the presence of a massive kapok (silk cotton) tree with great outstretched branches or a huge mampoo tree with extended and above-the-surface roots.

This pause was to give the spirit of the dead one in the coffin time to search the branches or the roots of the great

Massive silk-cotton tree, Henry Morton's Sketchbook, 1843–1844
(Courtesy St. Croix Landmarks Society. Owner of sketch: Lindsley R.
Bailey)

trees for spirits of friends or relatives, some long departed, who might now have joined an invisible audience waiting to greet the newcomer.

Plantation funerals for white folk was another matter. The death of a planter, or a member of his immediate family, caused an almost immediate cessation of all routine plantation activity as preparations were made for the interment.

For lack of a hearse, the coffin was generally carried on the shoulders of slaves from the mansion house to the cemetery, usually located on the estate. Negroes who were to be pallbearers were carefully selected based on time of service, loyalty, and closeness to the deceased.

Being a pallbearer to Massa, or Mistress, or their relatives, was a great honor. It gave such slaves a special status among their fellows, a status that was nourished and kept alive for a long time after the funeral (i.e. *"Remembah tis I who bury Massa!"*).

Because of excessive tropical heat and lack of refrigeration, the dead, regardless of rank, were hurriedly buried. There was little or no time for the modern practice of "viewing the body" under favorable conditions of embalming.

When a Lord or Lady of a Great House died, the body would be laid out for a matter of hours on a table in a cleared hall. Close relatives and friends, in deep mourning and dressed accordingly, sat on white cloth-covered chairs placed against nearby walls.

Inhabitants of the plantation — managers, overseers, and their families, bombas, field workers, household servants, grooms, stable-boys — were permitted to come by in a steadily moving line to "take a last look!"

Slaves, with straw fans, kept flies and insects away from the body and kept the air in the room circulating. Here or there, an attendant sponged the face and exposed limbs of the deceased with cold well water constantly supplied from the outside in metal containers.

These hurried West Indian burials had some side effects. In nineteenth-century planters' family records, it is not unusual to find expressed in letters and other documents fears of being buried alive!

Gentlemen and Lady of quality with 6 slaves in attendance (Author's private collection)

Planter's funeral (Author's private collection)

In these documents and letters, to be opened immediately at the writer's death, specific requests were made that in the event of such death, physicians or attendants be requested to cut deeply into the veins of the wrist or throat of the deceased to make sure that the dead were truly dead and not in a trance or coma.

One can imagine the nightmarish fears of such individuals of coming to in an earthern prison six feet under with no servants or slaves around to get them back to the surface. Some of these fears may have been generated from stories circulating on the plantations and repeated at the dining table, stories of funerals interrupted by noises inside the coffin.

One such tale concerned an Irish plantation manager named O'Haggerty who had seemingly died during the height of a drinking bout. When in the process of being solemnly taken to his final resting place, Mr. O'Haggerty came to from his "rigid hang-over" and found himself boxed in. Bellowing like an enraged bull, O'Haggerty created an explosion of excitement. The coffin was hurriedly placed on the ground and the lid raised. Up sat Mr. O'Haggerty with both fists clenched, filling the air with blasphemous oaths and demanding some alcoholic refreshments at once.

Another hair-raising tale that made the rounds of West Indian plantation society during the 1830's concerned the exploits of a bush doctor, Mongo Maud.

This woman, originally from West Africa, was noted for her knowledge of medicinal herbs.

In this particular instance, Mongo Maud had not been called to attend the sick but to preserve the dead, an art for which she had also achieved notoriety.

The wife of a prominent planter had died after a long and serious illness. The death had occurred in her husband's absence. He was due back on the plantation in a matter of days. The family was anxious to postpone the funeral until his arrival. Mongo Maud was sent for by messengers on horseback. At a designated area, a carriage with a team of spirited horses met her.

When the "bush specialist" arrived on the plantation, she brought with her several sacks full of dried leaves, twigs, and the cut bark of special trees. Enlisting the services of several muscular field laborers, she mixed her ingredients together then had them pounded in large mortars until they attained the consistency of a coarse powder. All of this was done in a matter of two or three hours. Then Mongo Maud laid down the law. If her work was to be effective, it was vital that she be left alone with the corpse. She wanted no one prying into her techniques. She guaranteed that when the husband arrived, the body of his wife would be in excellent condition.

Upon his arrival the husband found the body of his wife in *better* than excellent condition. She was sitting up in a chair in the room, pale and wan, but very much alive. The woman had been victim of a deep cataleptic trance. Under normal circumstances, she would have had a hasty burial. The absence of her husband and the steady and continuous stroking and anointing of her body by the skilled fingers of Mongo Maud had brought her back to life.

Sources

1. Rev. John Holmes, *Historical Sketches of Moravian Missions of the United Brethren for propagating the Gospel Among Heathen* (London: 1827).

2. David Cranz, *History of the Moravian Brethren*. Translated from German, Benjamin La Trobe (London: 1780).

3. John Lorentz Carstens, Manuscript, 198 pages. Danish Naval Library, Copenhagen. Prepared for the Danish King, Christian VI. 1742, Farumgaard. An eyewitness account of life among the Negro slaves of the Danish West India Islands of St. Thomas and St. John.

4. Krarup, Fr., *Jorgen Carstensen og Johan Lorentz Castenschiold, Fader og Son*. Personal historisk Tidsskrift, 2 raekke, bind III (Kjobenhavn: 1888).

5. Krarup, Fr., *Rettelser og Tillaeg til Artiklen om Jorgen Carstensen og J.L. Castenschiold*, Personal historisk Tidsskrift, 2 raekke, bind IV (Kjobenhavn: 1889).

6. Johan Lorentz Carstens or Castenschiold, Documents translated by Ulf Renberg, feature writer, newspaper Arbeiderbladet (Oslo, Norway: 1976).

7. Vore Gamle, Tropekolonier, *Dansk Vestindien*, translated by Elizabeth King (Copenhagen: 1952), II.

VIII
African Witchcraft Transplanted

In her study of customs and superstitions of the slaves of the West Indies published in 1834, Mrs. Carmichael, the British author, had this to say:

"The Obeah of the Negro is nothing more or less than a belief in witchcraft.

"There is not a single West Indian estate upon which there is not one or more Obeah men or women. The Negroes know who they are, but it is very difficult for white people to find them out.

"Obeah operates in the following manner. A Negro takes a dislike to another Negro, either upon the same estate or another. The disturbed or angry Negro goes to the Obeah man, or woman, and tells him or her that he will give money or something else as payment, if the Obeah man or woman puts Obeah on such a person.

"The Obeah man, or woman, then goes to the designated victim and tells him that Obeah has been put on him.

"In the greater number of cases, the mind of the victim is affected. The imagination becomes more and more alarmed. Lassitude and loss of appetite ensues. The spirit of the victim sinks. In many cases, death ends the drama.

"It is in vain to try to reason with the victim. 'Misses, they put Obeah on me. I know I gon' dead,' is all you can get out of him."

I.P.

In his extensive study of slavery in the West Indies (published in London 1807), Bryan Edwards had this to say about Obeah:

"By the term Obi-men, or women, is meant those who practice Obi. If we trace the origin of the term, we find that in the earliest of recorded time, a serpent in the ancient Egyptian language was called *Ob*.

"*Obian* was the later Egyptian name for serpent. Moses, in the name of God, forbade the Israelites to enquire of the demon Ob; or to have anything to do with his practices.

"The science of *Obi* was brought from Africa to the West Indies where it became very prevalent. The term Obeah denoted those practices of witchcraft, or sorcery, whereby certain Negroes by means of narcotics, potions or poisons made from the juice of plants or herbs, occasioned trances or death in other Negroes.

"Head Obi-men," continued Edwards, "were generally aged Negroes with hoary heads and stern countenances who played havoc upon the weak and credulous.

"The Negro masses feared them. Yet they resorted to them with implicit faith, calling on them for help in curing physical disorders, in predicting future events, in obtaining revenge for injuries and insults, or to help them discover thieves or adulterers.

"When a Negro was robbed of fowls, or hogs, or provisions, he applied directly to the Obeah-man or woman. It was then made known among his fellow blacks that *Obi* was set for the thief.

"As soon as the guilty one heard the news, he was terrified. No resource was left the thief but to confess and return the stolen items, or to enlist the superior skill of some more eminent Obeah-man, or woman, on his side.

"These Obeah-men, or women, carried on extremely lucrative trades, manufacturing and selling their concoctions, in all cases, at high prices.

"Obeah concoctions were usually composed of an assortment of materials: blood, feathers, parrot beaks, dog and cat teeth, alligator teeth, fish scales, lizard tails, frogs feet, broken bottles, grave-dust, rum and egg shells...."

"In regard to the common tricks of *Obi*, such as hanging up feathers, bottles, egg shells, in order to intimidate Negroes of a thievish disposition from plundering huts, hog-sites, or provision grounds, these were laughed at by whites but meant a great deal to simple and superstitious blacks, serving very much the same deterring purpose as scare-crows which are in general use among English farmers and gardeners.

"Midnight was a favorite hour to put Obeah in practice," Edwards noted, "and every effort and precaution were taken on the plantations to conceal these practices from white people.

"Deluded Negroes, who thoroughly believed in the supernatural powers of the Obeah-men, became willing accomplices in the concealment. The stoutest among them trembled at the very sight of the ragged bundle, the bottle, or the egg shells which were stuck in the thatch, or hung over the door of a hut, or upon the branch of a nearby tree to deter marauders."

Pere Labat, the French Jesuit priest, who spent much time in the West Indies, had this to say:

"The skill of some Negroes in the art of poisoning has been noticed ever since the early West Indian colonists became acquainted with them. The secret and insidious manner in which the crime is generally perpetrated, make legal proof of it extremely difficult. Suspicions have been frequent, but their detections rare."

Bryan Edwards continued:

"Many a slave uprising in the West Indies was only put down when the European authorities located the Obeah-man, or men, who had brought on the insurrection by furnishing the Negroes with magical preparations which were to render them invulnerable.

"The Obeah-man's power to cause such uprisings led to stern laws for the ultimate punishment by death of the inciter. The sight of an Obeah-man hanging from the gallows, dressed in his feathers and ceremonial garments, caused panic among his believers and stopped many a rebellion.

"At a place of execution, one of the leading Obeah-men defied the executioner, telling him that: 'It was not the power of white people to kill him.' The Negro spectators were greatly perplexed when they saw him die.

"Participants who were apprehended at the time of an upris-

Obeah-man's hut (Author's private collection)

ing were taken into closed and darkened rooms and shown images projected from hidden magic lanterns recently imported from Europe. These showings had an overwhelming effect. Not only did the lighted images, coming out of air, awe the agitators, but led to public declarations by them that the white man's magic was stronger than theirs."

In 1701, while Johan Lorentz was Governor, the French priest, Pere Labat, visited St. Thomas. The account of this visit, detailed in his work on the West Indies, *Voyage aux Isles de l'Amerique*, gives a fair picture of the state of the Danish colony at that time.

Among other interesting items which the Jesuit priest relates concerning the island of St. Thomas, is a story about an Obeah-man which was told to him by Monsieur Van Belle, managing director of the Brandenburg Company with its West Indian headquarters in St. Thomas.

A Negro slave convicted of Obeah and sorcery and of having made a little earthern figure speak was condemned by the judge of the island to be burnt alive. Van Belle happened to be in the path of the condemned man while they were taking him to the place of execution. Van Belle said to him, "Well, my fine fellow, you will never make your little figure speak again. They have broken it."

The Obeah-man replied, "It makes no difference to me, sir, I can make your walking stick speak to you if I will it to do so!"

This proposition astonished everyone. Monsieur Van Belle requested of the judge, who was present, to stay the execution in order to see if the Obeah-man could fulfill his boast.

The stay being granted, Van Belle gave his walking stick to the Negro who planted it in the ground and performed ceremonies around it.

The Obeah-man then asked Monsieur Van Belle what he wished to know from the walking stick. Van Belle replied that he would like to know if a vessel which he expected had left its port in Denmark on schedule. Also, just when would it arrive in St. Thomas and had anything happened to it during the voyage.

The Obeah-man, having repeated his incantations, retired a short distance and requested that Mr. Van Belle go closer to

Pere Labat, Jesuit priest (The British Museum, London)

the walking stick which would give him the answers.

This being done Monsieur Van Belle heard, to his astonishment, a little voice, clear and distinct, coming from the stick which said to him:

"The vessel you await has left Elsinore on such a day, Captain so-and-so commands it and there are such-and-such passengers with him. You will be content with its cargo and though it has passed through a gale of wind on its journey, lost a topmast and had its mizen sail carried away, it will anchor here before three days expire...."

Pere Labat does not say if any efforts were made to obtain a pardon for the Obeah-man for this remarkable performance. The priest concludes his account by stating:

"The Obeah-man was executed. The vessel arrived three days later as predicted. The statements coming from Van Belle's walking stick were verified to the letter."

Danish historians, almost without exception, seemed fascinated by tales of Negro witchcraft in the West Indian islands. In their writings, one finds an abundance of anecdotes dealing with such tales brought back to Denmark by ship captains, returning visitors and others who had heard these stories around the dining tables of the Great Houses of St. Croix, or from residents in the islands.

In 1840, for instance, the Danish Count Adam Moltke purchased from the Danish Crown the plantation on the northern coast of St. Croix known as *"Rust op Twist."* Translated from the Dutch this means: *"Rest after strife, struggle or toil."*

Rust op Twist estate is located in a valley surrounded by hills. At the time of purchase by Count Moltke it contained considerable land and more than 100 slaves, field workers and domestics.

Count Moltke had imported from Germany a spyglass of which he was very proud. Encased in brass and decorated with carvings, it was of latest design. Having but recently arrived, the Count had not had time to show the instrument off to his friends or to explain its use to his household staff.

One morning, a Negro slave girl, Mariah, on entering the parlor to do her customary cleaning, saw what she considered to be a headless apparition standing by an open window.

Actually, the Count was in the act of using his spyglass and in order to shut out the surrounding light, had covered his head with a black shroud from which the edge of glass protruded.

In a state of agitation, the young girl rushed back to the kitchen and reported that a *"jumbee without a head"* was in the parlor with a shiny thing sticking out from where his head should be.

Led by the head cook, an alarmed staff came to the door and saw Count Moltke in the act of returning a shiny object to its box.

"Are you alright, Massa? Mariah say she see a *jumbee in the room without a head!*"

Sensing what had happened, and in good humor, the Count declared that Mariah was correct. A *jumbee* had been there and had left him a *magic stick*. This *stick* told him that company was coming, was at that time a considerable distance away and would arrive at the plantation within two hours. Everybody should get back to his or her jobs of cleaning, cooking, and preparing to meet the guests.

As predicted, the company arrived within the time designated. Some came by horseback and others, a short time later, by carriage.

One of the kitchen help, a young apprentice to an Obeah-man on the estate, excitedly reported the incident to the witch doctor. The boy was duly instructed, under threat of disaster for non-compliance, to steal the magic stick and bring it to the Obeah-man as soon as possible. Finding the right moment, the apprentice performed the act.

It so happened that hours before, the Count had removed the large front lens of the instrument for cleaning and had neglected to put it back. Accordingly, the Obeah-man and the people around him, looking through the wrong end of the stick, found the world contracted to an alarming degree.

It did not take Count Moltke long to find out that his spyglass was missing. Immediately he called for his manager, overseer, and all slaves of the plantation and in the presence of one and all announced that his magic stick had been stolen.

Then and there, he issued a stern warning. If the stick was not returned by 12 o'clock midnight of the following night (full

Count Adam Moltke and friend (Courtesy St. Croix Landmarks Society)

Count Moltke and companion on grounds of his estate Rust op Twist, Henry Morton's Sketchbook 1843–1844 (Courtesy St. Croix Landmarks Society)

moon time), the illegal holder of the stick and his accomplices would be reduced in size until they would be no larger than crawling insects. By the following morning, the spyglass was returned to its rightful place.

Another witchcraft incident at La Grange plantation was more in the style of established Obeah practice. It involved violence and a black cat.

A young male slave, Obediah by name, belonging to La Grange estate, had been brought before the island authorities for brutally beating an old woman and almost killing her.

Obediah claimed that he had acted in self-defense since the old lady tried to put a spell on him through a black cat. He had narrowly escaped, and on the advice of another Obeah practitioner, had gone back to the old woman's hut to free himself of the cat's influence.

At first, Obediah was reluctant to talk. He seemed fearful of revealing the identity of the Obeah practitioner who had helped him overcome the spell. Once assured by the authorities that he did not have to identify his mentor, Obediah relaxed and spoke freely.

Late one afternoon as he was on his way from his labors in the field, he heard a strange sound of wailing to the accompaniment of a cat's mewing. The sounds seemed to be coming from a nearby hut. Curious, he left the trail and cut across a small field until he came close to the hut. Then it was that he got involved.

The door of the hut was wide open, and sitting there on the threshold was a very large black cat. As he looked at the cat and the cat looked at him, Obediah felt as if his strength was leaving his body. He found himself being drawn, against his will, right up to the doorway.

Obediah felt spellbound. His senses seemed to be reeling. The cat's eyes grew larger and larger and began spinning like wheels.

At that moment, there was a call from within the house, a strange voice, almost a croaking sound. The cat turned his head almost completely around and lifted his body to a standing position, as if to obey a command.

The spell was broken. Obediah forced himself away and like

La Grange Estate where Obediah worked, drawing by Frederick von Scholteu, 1833 (Sofarts Maritime Museum, Elsinore, Denmark)

Plantation Slob where Obediah went to get a powerful Obeah-man (Danish State Archives, Kobenhavn, Denmark)

a drunken man, staggered across the short field to the narrow trail, and with his limbs regaining movement, he made a wild dash away from the scene.

That night, and for several nights afterwards, Obediah's sleep was very disturbed. In his dreams he saw the black cat menacing him with his fierce revolving eyes, and in their depths he saw the gnarled and bony fingers of an old woman motioning him to come...come...come, and awakening, Obediah had to fight off a compelling urge to go.

Becoming more and more frightened, Obediah confided in friends and they advised him to go to a powerful Obeah-man who lived at Estate Slob.

Obediah went. The Obeah-man told him what to do. From past experiences, he knew the old woman and her formulas.

She collected black cats and when she had seven she boiled six of them thoroughly. Then she extracted their rib bones. Holding each bone up to a mirror, she saved those which did not reflect. These were the magic ones which she later dried and crushed and fed to the one surviving cat which developed strange powers and did her bidding.

The Obeah man advised Obediah to go to a tamarind tree, one that was heavy in trunk and with a full foilage. He instructed his client to select seven new shoots, three to four feet long and to tie them together securely to make a formidable whip.

Obediah was to go to the old woman's house as soon as possible, at the exact hour of the late afternoon as on the day in which he had had his original experience. Obediah was to walk boldly into the house, ignoring the cat. He was to go straight up to the old lady and say: "Maldina, Maldina, I have come to lash you!"

And without hesitation, he was to lash her, with all his strength, calling the number of each lashing, odd numbers, one, three, five, seven. He was to do this seven times for a total of 28 lashes, and *the spell would be broken!*

This is exactly what Obediah did. And he confessed to the authorities that he was not afraid of punishment because his mind was now at peace.

The beating of the old woman was part of the formula for extricating himself. Before the case was over, its ramifications had aroused the interest of the entire island.

The old lady died from the beating, and Obediah was deported from the island.

Sources

1. Mrs. Carmichael, *Customs and Superstitions of the Slaves of the West Indies* (London: 1834). A journalist and author, Mrs. Carmichael came to the West Indies in December of 1820, and returned to England in 1825.

2. Bryan Edwards, *History Civil & Commercial of the British Colonies in the West Indies*, 4th ed. (London: 1807).

3. Jean Baptiste Labat, *Nouveau Voyage aux Isles de l'Amerique* (Paris: 1724). Pere Labat visited St. Thomas in 1701. His memoirs give a lively account of conditions on the island at that time. The St. Thomas section of Labat's memoir was translated for us by Mr. Claude Caron, Consular agent of France to the U.S. Virgin Islands, 1965-1977.

4. James Smith, *Winter of 1840 in St. Croix* (New York: 1840).

IX

Plantation Opulence and Folk Tales

In the late 18th and early 19th century, the planter — slave economy flourished on the island of St. Croix. Great wealth and European influence combined to create a lavish lifestyle such as the landed gentry of the area had never before experienced.

I.P.

Portrait of Hans West (Fredericksborg Museum, Denmark)

Hans Birch Dahlerup, a young Danish naval officer, visited the islands in the early 19th century and was overwhelmed by the affluence which he witnessed, particularly in St. Croix.

He tells of the magnificent homes of the planters. They were like small palaces, he said, in which interiors and exteriors alike showed the fine handiwork of skilled architects and decorators imported from Europe. Money was no object, no deterrent to the creation of the finest styling.

The interiors of the great houses were the last word in exquisite taste: decorated ceilings, highly polished floors, gilded French mirrors, magnificent mahogany furniture, four-poster beds, finely wrought chairs, dining tables laden with the finest silver, crystal, and china. Nothing was missing to detract from a feeling and atmosphere of total elegance.

As for the exteriors, the plantation mansions showed the fine classic lines of Europe modified in design to suit tropical climate and outdoor living.

Dahlerup was impressed with the well kept grounds, the lush tropical gardens. As for the overall plantations, they matched in layout the best farms that Dahlerup had seen in Denmark.

Dahlerup, a popular and attractive young man, seemed to have had no trouble gaining entry to planters' homes. Time and again, he emphasized the quality of the aristocratic families with whom he mingled.

"They were fine and noble people, born and raised in immense wealth. Their handsome offspring, educated in Europe, showed the effects even more so than their elders: good breeding, the nicest party manners, aristocratic confidence in themselves and their society...."

The ballrooms in the plantation houses received special decorative treatment. During the social season, there were many balls and family parties. Then there were the *"lunatic balls,"* in which the imagination ran riot and the costumers and decorators outdid each other in preparing the weird, the grotesque, the comic, and the satirical outfits for the masqueraders and the setting for the ball.

But the most lavish celebration of them all occurred on the occasion of the Danish Queen's birthday. This was the high point of the season. It was held in the ballroom of the Governor General's mansion.

"The ladies were dressed in gowns from Paris and London," stated Dahlerup. "They wore jewels of a kind that were not even seen in the Royal balls in Europe. The men wore colorful uniforms or suits tailored by the foremost tailors in London and Paris."

Hans West, writing about St. Croix (1789-1790), tells of a visit to the Hogensburg plantation owned by a Danish planter friend, Johan Sobotker.

Hogensborg, which translated means "city of the hawk," was located on the north side of the Center Line road, 2-1/2 miles east of Frederiksted. It comprised tracts 17 in West End and 25 in Prince's Quarter.

West described the plantation house as a "small palace with well-arranged gardens. From the road a beautiful alley of stately palms led to the main building...."

West was especially excited about the well-kept stables and the dozens of spirited thoroughbred horses, Danish, Norweigan, British, and American. His friend, Sobotker, was an enthusiastic horse breeder and imported the finest stock for this purpose. With other planters having similar interests it was no wonder that the sport of thoroughbred racing reached a height in St. Croix.

Each participating plantation had its own house colors, its public backers, its well trained Negro grooms and jockeys. The tracks were beautifully laid out, with spacious grandstands, landscaping, and picturesque walks. A festive holiday spirit prevailed at these outings. People were gay and the costumes more so.

Dancing masters were brought from Paris and Vienna to teach those who had not lived, studied and frolicked abroad, the intricacies of the quadrille, the polka and other classical dances of Europe.

On occasions, tiring of the usual and the formal, there would be a sudden beating of drums, a signal to clear the dance floor, and the "Bamboula" would be presented to a delighted and excited audience.

From the beginning, the African slave had brought his music

Hogensborg Estate, by Frederick von Scholten, 1838 (Sofarts Maritime Museum, Elsinore, Denmark)

St. Croix plantation scene (Danish State Archives, Kobenhavn)

and his tribal dances with him to the West Indies. Richard Haagensen, a Danish observer, in a pamphlet printed in Kjobenhaven in 1758, *Beskrivelse over Eylandet St. Croix.* (probably the earliest printed book describing St. Croix), had this to say about the slaves and their dances:

"Drums sounded in the warm dark night and the jungle came to life again. . . . Here something was happening which the white people did not understand and which they feared. . . . At first the planters laughed at the monotonous music and the violent dances, but deep down they feared that this recreated jungle atmosphere might create rebellion . . . so they passed numerous laws forbidding these dances."

Laws or no laws, the Negroes found ways to keep their drum dances alive throughout the 18th century. Now in the beginning of the 19th century, many a young aristocrat returning from Europe with a sophisticated musical education began to search out and to publicly revive the African rhythms that had been transplanted to the Danish West Indies and had been repressed. On the top of the list was the "Bamboula."

Andre Pierre Ledru tells us a great deal about the "Bamboula" and its origins. Published in Paris, his lengthy study of habits and customs of the time appeared in two volumes under the title: *Voyage aux isle de Teneriffe, la Trinite, Saint Thomas, St. Croix et Porto Rico, execute par ordre du gouvernement Francais depuis le 30 Septembre, 1796 Jusquan 7 Juin, 1798, contenant des observations, etc. (Paris, 1810).*

According to Ledru, the "Bamboula" originated on the coast of Guinea. As it moved north, it became immensely popular among the colonists of North Africa and the Canary islands. Ledru first saw it performed in Teneriffe, largest of the Canary island group. He was visiting the capital, Santa Cruz de Teneriffe, when he saw the wild and savage dance.

Strange to say, it was not performed by Africans but by Spaniards. It was in the year 1801, and Ledru saw it performed in a church as part of a religious ceremony.

Ledru could hardly believe his senses that these violent, sensuous pagan manipulations of the body could be incorporated into catholic religious services. But there it was, happening right before his eyes.

Ledru stayed on for more, and during his period in Teneriffe, he saw the "Bamboula" performed again and again in church as well as in religious street processions. To add to the incredible, "the nuns danced it on Christmas night on a platform or theatre elevated in the yard of their convent, in front of the grating which was kept open for the public to see them...."

This "Bamboula Sacrie," of the nuns, according to Ledru, was in no way distinguished from the profane, except that no man was permitted to join in it. Belatedly the church, recognizing the physical and sensuous exaggeration of it, turned against the "Bamboula" and stopped it cold.

This was the dance that appeared in the elegant ballrooms of the Danish West Indian planters, the special treat for jaded appetities of cultured people saturated with the overly refined.

Specially selected teams of talented slaves performed the dance as no white man could. At times, however, some of the planters' children, trained by Negro teachers, delighted parents and friends by their close imitation and near mastery of the wild rhythms and body contortions of the African slave.

Yet another contemporary observer left a detailed account of West Indian plantation life.

During the 1820's, this young Englishman, Robert Ramsay, visited St. Croix and stayed as a guest at Schimmelmann's plantation, La Grande Princesse, in Christiansted.

In a letter to his family in London, dated February 16, 1823, Ramsay described the beauty of the estate, its splendid organization and management, the mansion house, its luxurious quality and furnishings, and intimate details regarding his host and family.

At the time of Ramsay's visit, a son and two daughters of the family had returned from Europe. Sent away in their early teens to finishing schools on the continent, these elegant children had returned to their West Indian home as gracious and cultured young adults.

Ramsay described a welcome home dinner-party for the youngsters at La Grande Princesse; chandeliers ablaze, crystal sparkling, heaping tables of delectable foods, beautifully dressed and elegant guests arriving in magnificent carriages.

Despite their acquired sophistication, Ramsay was impressed with the depth of feeling shown by these young people for certain household servants and plantation slaves, persons who had played an important part in their childhood.

It seemed to Ramsay that the youngsters showed as much devotion and deep feeling for these Negro domestics and slaves as they did for their parents and relatives.

Ramsay's observation was no rare phenomenon. Some years later (1834), an important and detailed study of social conditions of the white, coloured, and Negro populations of the West Indies was published in London.

The author, a British lady, Mrs. Carmichael, after a five-year study of human relationships in the West Indies, issued her findings. She, too, mentioned this emotional involvement between planters' children and plantation domestics and slaves.

"I have observed that when one servant in particular was selected for the children, within a short period that servant had twice the authority of either parent over her charges.

"I have seen many cases where the affection of the children towards one or more of the Negro domestics was unbounded; and where the children took no pains to conceal that they preferred the society of those servants to that of any white person.

"I have many times observed the children, upon going to bed, run to kiss those Negroes who were most about them, and say good night.

"I have seen children who are habitually rude upon contradiction, habitually kind to the Negro servants."

One of the links of affection between planters' children and their Negro nurses might be traced directly to storytelling. Some of the nanas on the plantations developed this form of entertainment into a fine art.

Of all the storytellers on St. Croix, none was more famous than Nana Bela of the western shoreline estate of Sprat Hall, near Frederiksted.

A member of the Bantu tribe of Angola, Bela had been brought to St. Croix as a young woman in a cargo of slaves. Almost immediately, she had been selected and purchased by the owners of Sprat Hall to be trained for domestic duties.

Bela had grown up and spent all of her adult years on the

McPherson children (The National Museet, Kobenhavn, Denmark)

Sprat Hall Estate, The Henry Morton Sketchbook, 1834–1844.
(Courtesy The St. Croix Landmarks Society)

estate. Now in her late fifties, she was a recognized member of the Sprat Hall establishment.

In 1833, when Sprat Hall was purchased from George Gordon Arvinger by the James McPherson family, a specific condition of sale was that Nana Bela remain with the estate.

As a storyteller, Nana Bela's variety of tales, her ability to express them, to convert African folklore into a West Indian setting, earned her a wide reputation. She was in great demand at garden parties for children which were well attended by grown-ups as well. A typical request for her services was as follows:

"The Countess Schimmelmann sends her compliments and best wishes to her dear friends (Mr. and Mrs. James McPherson) at Sprat Hall, and requests a great favor of them: to permit Nana Bela to attend a children's party to be held at Princesse estate (August 4, 1835).

"Many of our young guests have expressed a hope that Nana Bela and her stories will be in attendance.

"My dear friends, if you will grant this wish, a carriage will arrive at Sprat Hall at a designated hour to convey Nana Bela to our home...."

When Nana Bela arrived at La Grande Princesse, the children were waiting for her. Within a matter of minutes, Nana Bela was elevated to a seat of honor, with the children forming circles about her, eager for her stories to commence.

Generally, there was a set formula for the opening and closing of these tales. Each one started with the usual, *"Once upon a time..."* and ended with the phrase: *"Wheel ben (bend), the story en (end)"*. At each closing, the children would repeat this final phrase, *"Wheel ben (bend), the story en (end),"* in chorus, accompanied by a clapping of hands.

Here is a typical Nana Bela story:

An old lady named, Mama Luna, had left a pot of peas soup in her hut. When she returned, she found the pot empty. Somebody had stolen the soup.

The old lady's suspicions were divided between two children who had been playing nearby; and some plantation workers who generally passed her doorway. First, she tried out her song on the children:

"Pickaninnies, tis you who tief me?
Eat me peas soup and grief me?"
And the children answered:
"No, Mamy Luna, we no tief you!
Belly bawl, but we no grief you!"

Then Mama Luna went after the plantation workers. In order to reach their own estate, they generally assembled at the edge of a nearby river, and helped each other to get across.

Mama Luna got to them before they crossed and warned them to take care in trying to navigate the stream, for she had it in her power to cause the water to rise and drown the person who had stolen the contents of her pot. She wasn't out to punish anyone, but if the thief would confess, it was important to clear the innocent.

One and all denied the charge and several crossed the river without fear of danger, but upon the approach of a *belly woman*, (a pregnant woman), to the river's bank, she was observed by Mama Luna to hesitate:

"Why you stop, belly woman?
Tis you who tief me?
Tis you who grief me?
Tis you who tief me peas soup?"

The accusation upset the *belly woman* who marched right into the river singing as she went. (The woman's part is always chanted in chorus which the Negroes call: 'Taking up the sing!')

"If tis me who eat, eat,
Mama Luna's peas soup,
Drown me water, drown me,
Drown me head and drown me feet!"
And the old lady sang:
"Water, water, wet her feet
Belly big and belly cheat
If she tell me, let her floundah
If no tell me, pull her undah!"

The accused woman was obstinate. She continued to sing and to advance until she reached the middle of the river's bed, when down came a tremendous flood, swept her away, and she was never heard of again.

Mama Luna warned the other Negroes never to take the

property of another, always to tell the truth; and, at least, if they should be betrayed into telling a lie, not to persist in it, otherwise they must expect to perish like their companion.

In these islands, today, impersonal television has taken over completely from the "flesh and blood," very personal storyteller. Today's children sit for hours before this great detractor with eyes glued to the screen watching the too frequent synthetic and non-ending flickers.

This writer remembers, as a child, leaving the convent school with a group of other children and heading straight for Nana Mini to listen to her Bru Nansi stories.

Nana Mini lived in a small ground floor apartment on Garden Street. Her door was always open and we were always welcome. Nana Mini sat there, rocking away on her chair, the essence of kindliness and aged benevolence, ever ready to cater to our wishes.

We never went to visit her empty handed. Pooling our pennies, we knew just where to find Katie and her homemade West Indian candies.

Katie was based somewhere on Garden Street and very rarely did we have trouble locating her. A sharp-featured, very erect, accommodating woman, she would take the large wooden tray off of her head and let us make our selections.

Between the telling of her Bru Nansi stories, Nana Mini would pause for a candy break and would proceed to share her "goodies" with all those present.

There was quite a variety to choose from: "Jaw-bone," a light brown caramel stick; "Danish Girl," a pure white sugared stick encircled with a ribbon of red sugar; "Pinda," peanut sugar cake, a forerunner of todays peanut brittle (in retrospect, the "Pinda" was better). Then there were the homemade fresh coconut cakes which came in three colors, caramel, pure white or magenta red.

On occasions, we would not find Nana Mini at home, but there was always one of her innumerable godchildren to give us a message:

"Nana Mini say if you cum to tell you that Mr. Holst (the local banker), sen a bile (automobile), to take her to his house to tell him stories...." Whereupon, we would hastily climb the

Bank director Axel Holst's sitting room at Villa Santa Anna (*Aeldre Nordisk Architektur* Volume VI: Dansk Vestindien C.A. Reitzels, Boghandel, Kobenhavn, Denmark)

Entrance to Villa Santa Anna

Index

Acknowledgements

In expressing appreciation to those persons who helped with this book, it is my pleasure to start with three key individuals: *Marvin Galanty*, whose technical assistance and overall guidance were invaluable; *Barry Eisenberg*, designer, whose talents, applied here, are obvious and impressive; *Peter J. Malia*, editor, whose critical analysis of the manuscript combined with valuable suggestions were most helpful, as was his experienced help with the indexing.

Sincere appreciation goes, also, to Poul Erik Olsen, Danish State Archives, Copenhagen. Mr. Olsen's familiarity with archival material, his background knowledge of Danish history, events and people; his ability to secure permission for our use of pictorial material, were all of great help.

As regards translations from Danish documents, special thanks to Ulf Renberg, feature writer, Norwegian newspaper, *Arbeiderbladet*, Oslo; Elizabeth King, Copenhagen — St. Thomas; Steen Veedel, Copenhagen; Justus Paiewonsky, Oslo — St. Thomas; Gudney Pedersen, St. Thomas. Also recognition for Harold Larsen, National Archives, Washington (now deceased), for his very special help in locating important manuscript material in Copenhagen.

In the field of photography, thanks are due to Fritz Henle, St. Croix; Hillary Hodge, St. Thomas; Paul Paiewonsky, Oslo — St. Thomas. Also to Michael Paiewonsky and his Mapes Monde Co. Rome, for the use of prints and other pertinent material. Also special thanks to the St. Croix Landmarks Society for permission to use prints from the Reverend Henry Morton Sketchbook.

Thanks to Jens Peter Kemmler for his sketch of vessel *Polly* taking on slaves. Also the St. Thomas Daily News, editors & staff for their help and cooperation.